SERIALS COLLECTION DEVELOPMENT

LIBRARY MANAGEMENT SERIES

SERIALS
COLLECTION
DEVELOPMENT:
CHOICES AND
STRATEGIES

edited by
Sul H. Lee

Dean, University Libraries
Professor of Bibliography
The University of Oklahoma

THE PIERIAN PRESS
1981

Library of Congress Catalog Card Number 81-84645
ISBN 0-87650-136-6

THE PIERIAN PRESS
P.O. Box 1808
Ann Arbor, MI. 48106

For Melissa

Contents

Introduction

On May 21 and 22, 1981, a conference was held in Oklahoma City to consider the unique problems created by serials in the building and managing of library collections. The Conference on the Impact of Serials on Collection Development was attended by more than 90 librarians from the U.S. and Canada who listened and reacted to papers presented by experienced library managers on a number of important issues: the utilization of user surveys to assist in the development of journal collections; the marketing of collection development practices for serials; options in building and managing microform serials collections; serials budget management; serials de-selection; the Journal Access Service of the Center for Research Libraries.

The purpose of any conference volume is to provide a written record of the papers presented, as well as to be useful to the reader facing problems of a similar nature. Ideally, then, both theoretical and practical applications can be gleaned from the conference text. It is hoped that this volume will achieve these goals.

Unfortunately, this volume, like other conference publications, cannot convey the full sense of the meeting, including the unrecorded comments and discussion which are a key part of any colloquium. Librarians came to the conference at the Airport Sheraton Inn in Oklahoma City seeking answers to one of the most difficult and debated questions facing today's library manager: how best to acquire and manage a large serials collection. Not unexpectedly, discussion was lively, and provocative differences of opinion emerged. Yet the participants did agree on one important point: that librarians can no longer merely sit back and wait for serials problems to go away. In the end, the conference participants felt that they had gained something very useful from these papers and discussions: a better understanding of the problems of serials collection development, and a variety of approaches to consider in solving their own problems. It is hoped that the reader of this volume will also find something useful.

Six formal papers were presented at the conference, followed by a summary and reaction to the papers by a seventh speaker. The speakers and their papers were 1) Robin Downes (Director of Libraries, University of Houston), "User Surveys and Development of Journal Collections;" 2) Charles Osburn (Vice Provost for University Libraries, University of Cincinnati), "Marketing the Collection Development Aspect of Serials Control;" 3) Lester Pourciau (Director of Libraries, Memphis State University), "Development and Management of Microform Serial Collections;" 4) Herbert White (Dean, School of Library and Information Science, Indiana University), "Strategies and Alternatives in Dealing with the Serials Management Budget;" 5) Roger Hanson (Director of Libraries, University of Utah), "Serials De-selection: A Dreadful Dilemma;" 6) Donald Simpson (Director of the Center for Research Libraries), "The Expanded Journal Access Service at the Center for Research Libraries: Its Impact on North American Libraries." Reaction and summary comments were provided by David Stam, Andrew W. Mellon Director of The Research LIbraries, The New York Public Library.

This conference wàs made possible in large measure through the generous support of the University of Oklahoma Foundation and its Executive Director, Mr. Ron D. Burton. Mr. Burton was particularly instrumental in the Conference's success. I am personally indebted and grateful for his participation in the conference.

Several people contributed a great deal to the success of the conference itself and to the preparation of these proceedings. As Conference Coordinator, Mr. Rodney M. Hersberger played a key role in the meeting's success, arranging and planning conference facilities, preparing the conference brochure, coordinating registration, and performing a number of other important tasks. Mr. Hersberger also prepared the Bibliography and the Index which accompany the papers. He was ably assisted by Mrs. Pat Webb, secretary to the Dean of University Libraries. I would also like to acknowledge the editorial assistance of Robert Seal, Coy Harmon and Rodney Hersberger in the preparation of this conference volume.

Sul H. Lee
Norman, Oklahoma
September 10, 1981

JOURNAL USE STUDIES
AND THE
MANAGEMENT OF JOURNAL COLLECTIONS
IN RESEARCH LIBRARIES

Robin N. Downes

The invention of moveable type was looked upon by scholars in the medieval university as an instrument which would support and expand their influence. Historians of science point out that instead it so transformed the methods and costs of transmitting information that the medieval university was destroyed. A cultural revolution could occur over centuries then, and in decades now. Witness OCLC. Research libraries must deal successfully and quickly with issues of costs, technology, defining the market for their services, and delivering those services. These libraries do not have an unassailable position in supplying these services. One of the principal cost centers in research libraries is today out of control. A revolution equivalent to that created in bibliographic systems by OCLC must occur in the management of research library journal collections, and it must happen quickly. The problem is critical, but it can be resolved. The means are at hand. What are they? A discussion of the issues should begin with a review of the setting from which the problem has emerged.

The implicit philosophy which has guided the growth of research library collections in this century consists of one part fantasy, two parts pragmatism, and seven parts of undefined hopes and illusion. Research library collections have typically grown through a combination of large bloc purchases or gifts of thousands of volumes in which individual title decisions are inconsequential, and a gradual accretion through individual selection decisions in each of which a knowledge of a discipline and of a *constituency* has been assumed. The first can be disregarded and the second for the most part must be disbelieved. In the background as this ambiguous process unfolded in the great collection building years of this century has been the working philosophy that if a library spent enough emoney in a particular discipline and satisfied the perceived needs of faculty, a research collection of quality would result. History reveals that only a few libraries had the money, and whether rich or poor, few had a mechanism for determining faculty perceptions on a systematic basis.

1

For the first five decades of the century this philosophy appeared to be an acceptable one. As a working formula, it placed a quality book collection within the reach of a few wealthy universities and within the unrealistic ambitions of others. During the first half of the century, the success of this philosophy depended equally on the stability of costs of books and journals and the circumscribed limits of university research. Only historians have long memories, and most of us forget that until recently only a few major universities were primary sources of research for the nation. Only in those few universities were faculty judged primarily on their output of research publications. Success in building research library collections during this period was keyed to limited aspirations for the many, and for the few genuine research libraries a moderate balance between objectives and the dollars to achieve them. The methodology used by collection builders was based on pragmatism in the few wealthy universities and ill-defined hopes in the others. The lack of a mechanism for librarians to determine or predict faculty needs or perceptions on a systematic basis matched well with the faculty's perception of how scholarly research could be conducted. Among other qualities, that perception embraced the concept of a serendipitous and intuitive venture into the unknown. Thus the wealthy few responded to unpredictable needs by collecting almost everything, and the impoverished majority lacked both the fiscal resources and the demand for research collections.

The working realities of life always change before the guiding philosophy which supposedly underlies them. As in so many other things in life, the conditions under which research library collections are built have changed so drastically that the original guiding principles have become cosmetic. The volume of research publications, the economics of research libraries, and the spread of research as a condition of faculty success, have altered the original conditions of collection building beyond recognition. But with few exceptions the philosophy and methodology of building research library collections are still a composite of pragmatism and incompletely-defined hopes. The problem with pragmatism is its limited vision, and the result of ill-defined hopes is inaction.

These two themes can be detected everywhere in discussions of research library efforts to concentrate book and journal acquisitions on titles of predicted high or moderate value. It is in this context that surveys of journal use in research libraries have developed. Journal use surveys as conducted thus far can be understood best as a desperate compromise between the two themes of pragmatism and hope. Regardless of the techniques used by librarians and others to rank journal titles according to their level of use, the results have been imperfect and unsatisfactory when they have been applied to collection management. It is clear why, as we will see in a moment.

With this as background, it would appear inevitable that the management of journal collections would be buried in frustration. Until the correct premises are adopted, journal collections must fail to be an aggressively managed high-cost element of higher education. The reasons for past failures to manage these expenditures can be cited readily: inefficiency of access to journal titles which are of marginal values to a research library's constituency, and an inexact process of identification of marginal titles themselves. These are qualifying conditions of the design of journal use studies, and affect our judgment of their present and future value. These conditions are also a trap from which librarians have been attempting with futility to escape for decades.

We can break down this inefficiency of identification and access still further. First, no *predictable* source of a specific journal, or a source collection of journals defined by *discipline* and *scope*, has heretofore existed. The best a client could hope for was the location by a librarian of a specific journal in a remote location, and the unpredictable process of acquiring a copy could begin. These conditions limited both the efficiency of access and the ability to manage a collection. No agency with a defined range of journal coverage such as a National Periodical Center has been available to be used as a predictable reference point against which decisions to buy or not to buy a specific journal could be made. Second, there is the well-known document delivery problem. How long can a faculty member or graduate student be expected to wait to satisfy his/her curiosity as to whether an article in a journal not held by his/her library is (to begin with) even worth looking at? The answer — not long. The marvellous improvements in *bibliographic* access in the last ten years have highlighted the problem without supplying a solution. To know that a journal is available in fifty libraries from Kansas to Connecticut is like the second word in the term "good news." It is "news," but until rapid delivery of the document can follow, it is not *"good news."* It is instead a classic frustration model.

Scarcity of resources in the individual library, the lack of assured access to a defined alternative collection, and inadequate delivery time: that's inefficiency. With that as background, who can be surprised that research libraries burden themselves with marginal journals and watch with helpless paranoia as the journal budget eats into the ability to buy monographs. In the process of being painted into this corner, librarians have known that the most basic decisions on the nature of their collections were slipping further beyond their control each year, as basic economics of journal publishing shifted fiscal resources from the monographs budget into the journal allocation.

3

Against this background, the application of use surveys to journal collections has understandably had limited glamour. The results of an arduous research study has been an extension of inefficiency and frustration as access to additional titles has been shifted to a remote source. The librarians also have had the pleasure of justifying this transfer to a research library's most articulate and powerful constituency and the principal users of the journal collection, whose job security now depends on the production and publishing of research. If you want attention, raise an issue about the journal collection.

Something may finally be directing light on this dark picture. The Center for Research Libraries has made a conscious policy decision to expand its Journal Access System and even, it appears, at least to re-think its current policy of acquiring only infrequently used journal titles. The Center has joined OCLC, and OCLC's ILL system will in time be available. The seeds of a true access system are being planted. A collection defined by discipline, predicable availability from a dedicated collection, and quick document delivery. Even now, requests are being submitted by libraries to the Center via the same terminals used for searching data bases such as Dialog, and turnaround times of one week are becoming commonplace. These transactions equal access. Not interlibrary borrowing, not resource sharing, but access. Before this belated revolution can reach the streets and topple the statues, however, the Center will need time and money.

In these recent developments at the Center for Research Libraries are the potential for making access to infrequently used journals predictable and efficient. If this occurs as expected, it will make the study of journal use respectable, defensible, and necessary. Librarians who conduct such studies will have more to look forward to than an extension of inefficiency and frustration.

Any collection analysis project or systematic planning for collection development must now factor into its procedure the real potential for creating a "National Periodical Center" at the Center for Research Libraries. When should such systematic planning, based on this premise, be undertaken by research libraries? For the immediate present, there remains the option of pleading poverty in a book budget, to delay making hard decisions about journal selection and retention. But this avoidance technique carries a high price in the credibility of the library in the eyes of the faculty, and in the self-respect and morale of the librarians. The initiatives taken by the Center give reason to hope that it may not be necessary much longer to exact that price. But this will occur only if research librarians first understand the reason why the present system is ineffective and frustrating, second recognize that an opportunity is being created by the Center, and third support its Journal Access System, and urge its rapid expansion. One of the costs of such expansion may be an increase in the annual dues paid by members of the Center. There are many research librarians who believe that it is insufficient to talk only of membership *dues*. They are convinced that a major transfer of fiscal resources, if necessary from individual research libraries, to the Center is now appropriate.

If further reinforcement of this argument is needed, it can be found in those few studies of faculty response to assured journal access to remote collections. Studies of access to journals through MINITEX have, for example, revealed that researchers will use with minimal frustration an assured system of rapid access to a predictable source of journal articles.

I have asserted that journal use studies are made respectable by these emerging new conditions. Do the altered conditions have an impact on the relative utility of certain types of use studies?

Journal use studies fall easily into several categories. The most commonly applied methodology relies on gross measures of actual use of specific titles in a single library. These studies are usually performed alone, but are sometimes combined with a ranking of titles by library users (usually faculty) in terms of essential, moderate value, and marginal value. Both types of use studies are typically performed separately for each discipline, are limited in sophistication of analysis, and are linked to short-term, one-time projects to reduce expenditures for journals in a specific library.

Reviewers of studies of gross measures of actual use have commented on the difficulty of obtaining reliable data. Journal use surveys have produced gross figures on volumes picked up from tables, removed from shelves and reshelved by the user, and circulation data if bound volumes circulate. But such studies supply negligible inferences on the importance of a unit of use to the user. Was it a purposeful use with a valuable result, or a casual use with no significant result? Nevertheless, when combined with surveys in which faculty are asked to rank the importance to them of journal titles, such journal use studies *can* provide a very *approximate* measure of the relative level of use and the quality of that use in a group of journal titles in a discipline.

Citation analysis, a third methodology, has attempted to fill the need for measuring the relevance or impact of a journal by, as we know, measuring the number of ctitations to articles in the journals in a discipline. The technique has been widely used and reports in the literature are numerous.

Citation analysis has been conducted most often as a study of journal use and value for a discipline generally, and to a much lesser degree as a method of measuring journal use in specific libraries. A persuasive case has been made for using citation analysis only to generate core lists of journals, ranked by frequency of use, so as to assist individual libraries in developing local core lists of essential journal titles. Although the case has been aruged from both sides, the strongest argument is for using such core lists as only one of many indicators of journal value in a secific library. The argument will in any case quickly be recognized as unrealistic by practitioners, since the number and strength of influences on journal selection *and retention* in specific libraries makes the decision-making process so complex that reliance on a single authorty is inconceivable.

Other studies have attacked the validity of citation analysis in making local decisions on journal rentention by noting that citation analysis is by its nature oriented to single disciplines. Its validity in predicting use in multi-disciplinary library collections is as a result seriously in question. One reviewer states categorically that only measures of journal use derived from a local use study are of any practical value to librarians. Most critics agree that citation analysis generates interesting results but is unreliable as a direct predictor of the level and impact of journal use in local situations.

A fourth approach to decision-making for journal selection and retention has been taken in the efforts of researchers to supply cost models for a core collection of journals of optimum size and level of use. Cost models have been developed by Buckland and Woodburn, Brookes, and Leimkuhler. All of the cost factors in maintaining a journal collection are combined in these cost models, including subscription costs, binding, check-in, and related costs. Added to the resulting fixed costs are the variable costs of interlibrary loan, which depend on the size of the core collection and the demand for journals not included in it. The value of these cost models for a library which wants to create a core journal collection of high use titles remains a luxury few can afford, of doubtful reliability, and of even less credibility in a typical academic library setting.

A fifth methodology is the collection analysis project in which the research and instruction environment is described, and policy statements and standards are adopted to guide collection growth and decisions are retention of individual titles.

It is the argument of this paper that the existence of a National Periodical Center (by whatever name it is designated) will simplify and clarify the choice of a methodology to be utilized in an individual library for surveys of journal use. Assured access offers faculty as well as librarians a simplified set of choices. In this environment, it would be helpful if studies leading toward the development of a core collection of journals in each discipline could be undertaken by library researchers at the profession-wide level. Citation analysis could well be one of the methods used to develop these core lists. If citation analysis is used, it is of course a ranked list which results.

The Center for Research Libraries should develop corollary journal lists to complement those developed for individual libraries.

A key point to make about such ranked lists is that citation analysis depends for its validity on a statistically significant number of citations. When the list reaches down to the lower depths of journal use, the rankings don't mean much because the citations are negligible in number. On the other hand, unless the ranked list includes marginal journals, and defines them as such, its usefulness as a device for justifying retention or elimination of specific titles is reduced.

My argument is again that each research library should undertake a systematic study of the use of its journal collection. Journal costs have forced the issue. Research libraries must establish now a set of benchmarks for the journal collection in each discipline. They must reflect today's reality in the needs of faculty and graduate students. Such benchmarks already exist in cursory form in many research libraries. They may consist of a listing of criteria for selection and retention with brief definitions of each. Such a level of collection analysis often is concealed under a label such as "Guidelines for Serials Selection and Cancellation." Regardless of the candor with which it is labelled, any collection study which involves librarians and faculty in joint systematic decision-making on the content of the journal collection is a collection analysis project. The weakness of the cursory approach is the fragility of the benchmarks which result. Obviously this affects the credibility of the retention decisions made on the strength of the analysis. The argument in this case is in favor of the most complete collection analysis for the journal collection which local resources make possible.

The factors to be considered in any level of journal collection analysis include the same principles, regardless of the scope of the study.

They include the following:
- Relation to curriculum and research;
- Relation to the total collection;
- Reputation of publisher and contributors;
- Breadth and quantity of demand;
- Cost;
- Indexing in standard sources;
- Accessibility from other sources.

These assertions can be made in conclusion:

Each type of journal use study accumulates only one or at most two of the measures of value and impact of a journal title. None can be used alone as the dominant element in a decision on retention.

Measurements of actual journal use are open to distortion by the difficulty of obtaining reliable data. Such results are also subject to question as to the quality or impact of use.

As a technique for measuring journal use, citation analysis performed locally is costly and difficult, assumes a level of bibliographic control of campus research which is unusual and relies on a sample too small for reliability.

Citation analysis performed at a discipline-wide level for general use is potentially more useful than locally conducted surveys. The ranked lists which result are only one of a number of elements to be weighed in a decision on retention. The chief value of a ranked list lies in its potential for development of a model core list of journals, which individual libraries can then adapt to a specific situation. The Center for Research Libraries should develop corollary lists within its defined area of responsibility. Such core lists are of most value if they are comprehensive enough to rank marginal journal titles, since it is these titles whose exclusion from local core lists must be justified.

Each research library should perform a systematic analysis leading to the development of a core collection of journals. Such a collection analysis should be coordinated with the evolution of the Journal Access System of the Center for Research Libraries into a National Periodicals Center.

It is long past time that librarians stopped talking about conventional resource sharing for journals when our everyday experience shows that it is cumbersome, unreliable, and frustrating to borrow from other libraries. Access to the journals in the collection of the Center for Research Libraries is much faster, the result more predictable, and the frustration level less. If a faculty member asks a retail firm to order a consumer product and is told that it may take months and delivery cannot be assured, he or she may be excused for taking his or her business to another firm. This is the right time to take the research library's needs to the Center for Research Libraries and give them our business. We should do so even if our membership fees have to be very substantially increased. Resource sharing has not been emphasized previously in this discussion because for the purpose of cost control and the management of journal collections it doesn't work.

The objective of journal use measurement, citation analysis, core journal lists, and collection analysis, is the successful management of a cost element of research libraries which is now out of control. The genuine possibility of reaching this objective makes these methodologies respectable options for the management of journal collections. The crisis in the management of journal collections can be resolved, using programs and methodologies which are within our grasp.

8

MARKETING THE COLLECTION DEVELOPMENT ASPECTS OF SERIALS CONTROL

Charles B. Osborn

Introduction

The question "What are you doing about your serials?" is posed with such frequency these days that an observer from outside our profession might justifiably suspect serials to be a most troublesome, yet socially acceptable, disease. After all, everybody has it. One must agree that our serials problems are both common and quite serious, but I wish to suggest that these problems do not themselves constitute the disease; they are, instead, symptomatic of a more profound malaise from which our attention should not be diverted. The theme of the present paper evolves from a diagnosis of what I believe to be the real problem and a prescription for corrective therapy.

In essence, university libraries traditionally have claimed to be responsive to the needs of their respective communities, which is to say, the scholars at all levels who make up the academic institution. Although these libraries did maintain the appearance of responsiveness for a couple of decades, they really were in the process of developing rather independently of their local scholars. When funding levels no longer adequately supported this force for independence, a number of latent problems began to surface, the serials problem not the least among them. Proper, effective working relations between library and university had been supplanted, if they ever existed at all, by the subtle force for independence, and now, almost suddenly, this direction must be reversed. The adjective "responsive" is particularly interesting in this connection. I think that its commonly understood meaning when applied to the role of libraries suggests that role to be passive. Contrary to that interpretation, the major strain in the increasingly baroque theme of this paper is that, while university libraries must become more truly and manifestly responsive to their communities, responsiveness, for this purpose, must be characterized by an aggressive, proactive role in university library management.

If it begins to sound as though I have already strayed from the main topic of serials just so I might better grind a favorite axe, that is not so; for, in considering a more pragmatic relationship between the community and the library, it is important to bear in mind the increasing centrality of scholarly and scientific journals in today's academic enterprise. It is worth a little time at this point to emphasize this particular notion, because it should be clear that, if we have problems with the inflating number and price of serials, those problems are very seriously complicated and raised to a higher level of significance by their growing importance to scholarly communication. To understand the changing significance of journals one need only consider the following trends: the increasing interdisciplinarity of scholarship; the resulting increase in specialization; the rapidity with which the frontiers of knowledge are advanced, largely because of technology; the influence of competition for recognition and for research dollars; and the expansion of academic interest in societal matters of the moment and of the future. So far, the best scholarly medium for the accommodation of these trends is the journal, and that medium is used very heavily. My conclusion to all of the above is that we are moving from a predominantly book based kind of service organization in academic libraries to one that may be based heavily on technology in the future — that remains to be seen. In the meantime, however, we are in an interim stage, wherein we are predominantly journal based, and becoming ever more so. Consequently, just as most of us probably think that we could get our budgets in control if we could only control serials, I would add to that that we could very likely develop an enlightened relationship between library and community, generally, if we could do so on the basis of serials.

We are all pretty much aware of the impact that scholarly publication patterns have had on our acquisitions budgets and on our overall budget planning, especially in the general economic environment of the past decade. The events went something like this. The prices of books and journals escalated more rapidly than any other higher education cost, except for energy in the most recent years. Journal prices inflated at an even faster rate than those of books, while scientific and technical journals, whose base price was already higher than the base price of most other kinds of journals, inflated even more rapidly in cost than those others. At the same time, the rate of growth in new titles of journals outstripped the publication rate of new books. In many university libraries, this situation was reflected in the acquisitions budgets by a growing proportion of budget being occupied by serials and by a growing proportion of the serials expenditures being occuped by science and technology journals. It became clear to those of us who are intrigued by exaggeration that the logical conclusion to this trend line would be that our libraries would eventually find affordable no books at all and only one journal, and that it would be a chemistry journal. To make matters worse, we learned by experience that our efforts to control the monstrous serials problem by cancellation were characterized by cancellation of the least expensive titles, which were replaced very shortly by a greater number of new titles costing far more, title by title, than those cancelled. This may be an oversimplification of what has been happening, but I believe that it is, by and large, a fairly accurate synthesis.

The point I am trying to make by outlining the evolving significance of journals to academia and, at the same time, the complex budgetary considerations implied by the publication statistics of serials, is that the area of overlap between these two spheres of activity presents itself as traveled, but not well charted, territory for exploration. The goal of this exploration, I believe, should be the formulation and testing of new administrative concepts, aimed at a restructuring of the relationship between the library and the academic community, concepts that are based on substance of significance to both spheres. An essential part of this concept of administration, which I will outline subsequently, holds that librarians must and can take the initiative in influencing academic planning and that the policy on serials selection is a natural focal point for doing this.

If done well, both academic planning and serials control function as ongoing processes requiring a balance of strategies to meet both immediate needs and long term goals. Both efforts require a high degree of organization among conflicting forces; both require regular and systematic evaluation; and both require hard trade-off decisions. The maintenance of an academic program has definite budgetary implications for the future, as does commitment to a serial. These are some of the essential similarities of academic planning and serials control, and one could go so far as to observe that a scholarly journal is to the library as an academic program is to the university. For these reasons, I think that the marketing of the collection development aspects of serials control to the university faculty is both necessary and quite manageable.

Definitions

In spite of my humanist's aversion to the term "marketing," I have to concede that its meaning for management experts has expanded today to incorporate activities and concepts that we all would probably agree are essential to successful library administration

11

of the future. For example, among them are the following: marketing aims at satisfying the user, thereby achieving organizational goals; marketing research establishes the overall size and structure of the market, identifies user characteristics, assesses needs of the users, and interprets trends in the market; marketing strategies include the development of overall plans to maximize impact on the market in both the short and the long term, decisions on which products and services to offer, and the establishment of standards and of measures of performance.

We need only substitute the words "academic community" for "market," and the direct applicability of these efforts to libraries is very evident. One encyclopedia of management offers a definition that summarizes the characteristics of marketing in a way which, in spite of the clumsy wording, I find particularly significant for our purposes. "Marketing may also be perceived as a vast communications system, giving information regarding product availability to consumers while feeding back data regarding consumers' wants to producers." The points I want to make in concluding this definition are that marketing is considered a creative management function; that we certainly could be more creative than we have been in library administration; that we need to adopt the management attitude of giving serious, concerted attention to strategies for making our organizations important to our communities; and that this should be accomplished in much the same way that business is doing it, which is to say, by creating what really amounts to a new dimension in academic library administration. In any case, the activities and concepts outlined above in definition of "marketing" are closely akin to those embodied in the definition of collection development I advocate.

That definition is as follows: Collection development is a public service system, which is effected through a decision-making process that leads to a determination of the acquisition and retention of materials. The first key concept in this definition is that collection development is a public service. Any organized effort in the library to meet the public need by working directly with the public to determine how best to meet that need is a public service. Collection development should be, but rarely, if ever, has been, our most public of services, for it is the main connection between the community we serve and the library; it is the active expression of a library's *raison d'etre.*

The second key concept embodied in this definition of collection development is that of system. The idea that collection development is a public service *system* is especially crucial, because it implies that there is a whole whose parts are moveable yet highly interdependent. The idea of system implies that collection development is not a specific action, but rather that it is dynamic, that it has a benerating force or forces, and that anything put into or taken out of the system has some kind of impact on the system as a whole. Organically, the system is a sphere of influence that overlays a meaningful bond between collection development and the community and a meaningful bond between collection development and the rest of the library's services and operations. Collection development processes drive the system both where it touches the public and where it touches other services and operations in the library. Toward the end of this paper, I intend to return to the concept of system in collection development, because there are some aspects of this that warrant elaboration.

The next concept incorporated in my definition of collection development is that of the decision-making process, and I wish to place special emphasis on the word "process." This process is the specific element of energy that drives the system, for it both informs and is informed by the community about the relationship between goals and needs, and informs and is informed by other library operations and services about goals and parameters. The word "process" means that information becomes knowledge through experience, and that this is layered or made cumulative, always providing context for subsequent cycles of the process. Process is, in itself, a learning experience that should translate from a continuous testing of policy, plans, operations, and services against a constant flow of information about the academic community. In a narrow sense, the end of a cycle in the decision-making process of collection development is achieved with the selection or weeding of certain materials, but in a broader sense that decision re-generates the collection development system. With these definitions in mind permit me, then, to repeat my overall working definition of collection development: It is a public service system, which is effected through a decision-making process that leads to a determination of the acquisition and retention of materials.

The next key word in the title of this paper is the word "serials." However, for the sake of brevity and simplicity in the face of what some might consider an already motley array of working definitions for serials, I suggest that we focus primarily on scholarly journals. By use of the word "control," I am referring, of course, to the power or authority to guide or manage. When we consider the range of possibilities for "control" in the context of marketing collection development, however, it is useful to consider other meanings; for example, that which includes skill in using a technique, or the monitoring connotation of control, or the definition that refers to control as a mechanism for activating, regulating, and guiding a system. Since control of serials seems to be the theme of today's lecture series, then we should explore the major goals we might hope to achieve through control.

Goals of Serials Control

The potential span of control over the collection development aspects of serials is far-reaching. It ranges, for example, from bibliographic control for purposes of selection decisions, through selection policy control, budget control, and space control, to the exercise of influence over the publishing industry. If we combine the concepts and activities considered thus far through the definitions of marketing, collection development, and control, some specific kinds of goals within that spectrum become evident.

It may actually be true that, if only we were able to control the serials budget, the remaining acquisitions budget would be manageable. Books are less apt than journals to be the objects of urgent demand, and are more likely candidates for our present interlibrary loan services. Similarly, in cases of cooperative development of collections, the multiplicity of books and their distinctive characteristics as individual units make them suitable for division of responsibilities by large blocs than do journals. Control of the serials budget is, therefore, a logical goal.

Another obvious goal would be to control the physical growth of the journal backfiles because of their steady and rapid encroachment on space, and the constant handling they require during stack shifts. Weeding is one method of a achieving this goal, whether it is weeding for discard or for transfer to some other facility or agency either for storage or central deposit. However, even prior to this, an important goal would be that of establishing a process to ensure that not only the right titles are added to the collection, but, more specifically, that they are in the most appropriate format. By format, I mean traditional microform versus hard copy; but I am also referring to options of online services which are likely to take on more of the characteristics and substance of today's journals.

The nature of the serials collection itself provides several areas for goal setting. Most general among them is the determination of an appropriate balance in expenditure between serials and books. This is an important guideline for the selection and cancellation processes, and the identification of an appropiate balance by broad subject area is an especially useful exercise in understanding the configuration and the use patterns of the literature, with a view to the establishment of solid academic principles and priorities behind budget management. In that connection, a very clear goal is the assurance that the right persons are involved in determining the appropriate balance between books and journals and, within that division, determining which titles are the most important for that particular university.

Just as journals are largely representative of the dynamism of scholarship, through the dissemination of discovery, invention, creativity, and reinterpretation, so the journal collection, in the aggregate, should reflect the overall dynamism of the academic library. Accordingly, a goal of serials control would be always to allow room for the addition of new titles, even in the worst of financial times. This relates directly to another goal of serials control, which is the establishment and continuous revision of a definition, in local terms, of a core subscriptions list. The definition of a core is essential to good internal communications within the university and to communications linking one library to another in cooperative programs of collection development. It seems to me that adoption of the core concept is fundamental to any kind of acquisitions budget control that is intended to be guided by academic priorities and principles and, conversely, that academic planning can be informed very pragmatically by an understanding of the local application of this concept.

The ultimate, long-term goal of serials control must be the achievement of a sense of cooperation between faculty and library. This should be based on a mutual understanding of goals, methods, limits, motivations, expectations, and plans, so that library development becomes closely integrated into the institutional consciousness, while the library enhances the information base of its administration. I believe that the time is now ripe for this kind of linkage to be successful. Higher education is expressing an unprecedented interest in scholarly communication and, in doing so, is beginning to concentrate attention on libraries. Similarly, academic libraries seem to be moving toward client or community-oriented concepts of service, away from a primarily collection orientation. It is within the province of librarianship to take the leadership in realizing the potential of the organic whole that joins the library and academia, but, by definition, academic librarianship will have to adopt a more aggressive and explicit program to do this than has been its custom.

Intelligence Based Administration

I have suggested that serials control is the substantive area of university library administration that affords the most direct and meaningful connection to the faculty. In that sense, serials control is not simply an end in itself, but is rather a means of moving toward a larger goal. One generalization about the past is that collection development in university libraries treated serials as though they were somewhat automatic additions to the collections. Largely because of the strong influence of traditional values and ideals in collection development, most energies and attention were diverted from serials to development of book collections, and serials tended to be viewed as the faculty's realm of responsibility. This trend, along with budget arrangements for serials that have existed, and perhaps persist in some libraries, supported the "automatic" connotations of serials development. Moreover, it appears that university library administration did not pay very much attention to collection development, generally, until the acquisitions budget was launched on a collision course with the rest of the economy. Now we are looking for ways to gain control; but we are doing so in a new era, one which is so complex in its technological, social, economic, and political implications for change that our judgment is extraordinarily dependent on a very broad base of diagnostic and predictive information. We have been able to get away with a lot of independence in collection development because of adequate levels of funding, because of our naive sense that library users in an academic setting could by and large manage fairly well on their own, and because alternative formats and substitute sources were limited. However, with the proliferation of journals and the imminence of innovative ways to convey journal-type information through advanced communications technology, the latter rationale is no longer any more applicable than are the former.

At the same time, it is becoming evident that we are now expected to be responsive to, and therefore important to, our public if we are to continue, not as an anachronistic appendage, but as a vital organ (dare I say "heart") in our society and within our institutions. It is no longer merely a question of budget that gives us difficulty, it is more a question of how the library should relate to the rest of the university. On a positive note, the expanding universe of materials controllable by the library is conducive to a greater potential for the library to address the the needs of those who have not been library users in the past. Should we academic librarians fail to seize this opportunity to address total community needs, including those of the traditional non-user of our libraries, the consequences for our profession will be serious, and rightly so.

We need to know more about our community, both library users and non-users; what their needs are, what their motivations and goals are; what their learning and information seeking habits are; and this should be translated into a new kind of information base for collection development policy and procedure. Since my view of collection development places it at a pivotal position between library and community and at a central position in library operations, then we are talking about an understanding of the sociology of our community informing a system for the provision of resources, as the underlying structure of library administration. The chief activity involved in this kind of system is described best by the word "intelligence."

"Intelligence" used in this sense means, of course, information gathering for strategic purposes and planning. It is an old military term that is particularly applicable to library administration for several reasons: Intelligence is an offensive maneuver that is most effective when unobtrusive; it applies to a community whose patterns of behavior affect us; it assumes that an understanding of the community's pattern of behavior and motivation is essential to planning and to the determination of strategic offensive moves. Similar to military intelligence, academic library administration deals with a complex community over which it has no authority and only indirect influence. An advantage of academic library administration over military intelligence, at least in potential, resides in administration's capacity as colleague of the target group to exert influence.

Conclusion

I would probably do well to apologize for recommending the application of these marketing and intelligence approaches to serials control, since I am also advocating their development into a dimension of university library administration whose definition would place academic librarianship somwhere between a beleaguered marketplace and a war zone. However, the goals, definitions, and strategies all seem to fit, and they do, perhaps, afford us the opportunity to look at what we are doing, and trying to do, from an altered perspective. There is no single new idea in any of this, of course, unless it is the theme that some of our largest present and likely future problems can be reduced to manageable size by first emphasizing strategies to integrate the library into the mechanism, if not into the mind, of the university. Emphasis on strategy in this case might well be translated in both business and military terminology as a campaign, and if I may continue these loose analogies, an ongoing campaign to maintain an intelligence system for library administration could yield great profit for both university and library, rendering both victors.

Permit me, in closing, to repeat my belief that there is a very useful sociological system waiting to be discovered, and that we have not yet tested to full potential the administrative tools of discovery.

DEVELOPMENT AND MANAGEMENT OF
MICROFORM SERIAL COLLECTIONS

Lester J. Pourciau, Jr.

The financial retrenchment which has affected all of higher education for several years has had a detrimental effect on college and university libraries. This, of course, is self-evident. Equally evident is the deterioration of the ability of libraries to develop and to maintain quality collections. This deterioration, particularly their ability to deal adequately with inflation in the cost of serial subscriptions, has put many libraries in the uncomfortable position of speaking only in a rhetorical sense about *developing* collections, and has forced them to deal primarily with the vexing problem of merely *maintaining* existing serial collections. Thus, this conference and our presence here.

One of the ways in which libraries can combat the problem of serial subscriptions cost inflation is to consider acquiring and maintaining certain serials in microform. My remarks today will be limited to this consideration and, more specifically, will be limited to the development and management of retrospective journal collections in microform format. From the onset, you should know that I have no panacea to offer you, and that I will not try to persuade you that it is less expensive to buy and to maintain journal collections in microformat than it is to build paper copy collections. Rather, I will speak largely from an experientially based point of view, and will elaborate on the many factors which need to be considered when embarking upon a microfrom journal collection experience. Associated with each of these factors is a certain cost, but I will refrain from discussion of precise costs because of the variation in these caused by different circumstances in different libraries in different geographical regions.

As a point of reference, it might be good to give you a brief description of the microform collection with which I am experienced, and some idea of how this collection fits, organizationally, within the library I represent. It is housed, for the most part, in one large room of some 7,000 square feet in the main library building at Memphis State University. It includes more than 1.6 million pieces of micro-material of which slightly less than 300,000 are reels of 35mm film. Included in this figure of 300,000 are approximately 1,200 periodical titles for which current subscriptions are held, but which are not bound. Rather, microfilm copies of the most recent, full bibliographic volume of these are added to the microforms collections as they become available. There are some titles which are located in branch libraries and which are converted to microfilm as opposed to being bound, but these are few in number. The microforms reading room contains eighteen 35mm film readers, nine fiche readers, and two ultrafiche readers. There are also two reader/printers for film and two fiche printers included in the equipment. Completing the complement of equipment is a cleaning machine for film and fiche.

Development of a Journal Microform Collection

A simple enumeration and discussion of factors germane to developing journal collections in microform is the best and most expedient way to discuss the topic, and among the first to be considered is that of attitude toward microforms. Some persons do not like microforms and some, if not many, of these persons are librarians.[1] Among the reasons heard for opposing microforms are eye and body fatigue associated with reading microforms, poor quality of photography, poor reproduction capability, and poor reading areas. There is some truth to each of these reasons, but frequently they are overstated and are based on experiences with microform collections and reading areas which do not have assigned to them an adequate priority within a particular library. The point to be made here is that the success of any commitment to microform journal collections will be determined, in large part, by the attitude with which librarians approach the commitment. This matter of attitude will have an impact on most of the other factors I will discuss and, thus, will be a major determinant of ultimate user satisfaction.

Space is a particularly important factor associated with success with microforms. The library that relegates a microforms collection to a location which is unattractive, not easily accessible, uncomfortable, or is in other ways less than desirable, is not giving the collection a fair chance and cannot reasonably expect its microforms venture to be a successful one. Microform collections reduce by 90 to 98 per cent the space required to store and retrieve material previously stored on paper,[2] and this presents a great temptation to librarians to crowd them into space otherwise undesirable for storage of other material. This is unfortunate because the design and administration of a microform area to provide a comfortable physical and psychological environment is a fundamental variable of user acceptance of, and the success of, a microforms collection.[3] Ideally, space allocated to microform use should be easily accessible within the library, aesthetically pleasing to the user, and lighted so as to reduce eye strain to a minimum. Further, it should be furnished with reading stations which are as physically comfortable as possible.

Among the frequently cited advantages of microfilm is security of whatever is stored on film in the sense that it is difficult to alter or to mutilate images on film. The security of the film itself, and by this I mean its susceptibility to theft or other loss, is a different consideration. To minimize theft or loss, the space used for a microform area should lend itself to an arrangement such that users do not have direct or ready access to the actual film collection. More comments on the implications of this will come later.

The preceding comments suggest very clearly a considerable allocation of effort, time, and money to the development of a microform collection. But with library building costs increasing as they are, the incentive to use for microforms only 10 per cent or so of the space which would otherwise be required for paper copy is not merely attractive; it is compelling. There is little or no doubt that a careful identification of the costs associated with the establishment of a microform area as I have suggested would yield a total figure substantially less than the aggregate of those required to provide space for a collection of paper copy.

Questions about equipment needed to develop a microform collection are especially subject to local considerations because of the uneven availability of maintenance. Further, the number of pieces of reading equipment required will have to be determined by the size of the population being served by the library, the size of the microform collection, and the level of use. The cost of reading and reader/printer equipment, apart from special or package deals, and initial freight or shipping charges, will be similar, but the choice of equipment will be determined in part by the cost and availability of maintenance. Typical maintenance contracts provide for preventive maintenance with added charges for service calls. I will suggest here, parenthetically, that it is wise for a library to consider the purchase of a few, simple hand tools and to employ, among the microforms staff, someone who has a knack for simple repair and adjustment of reading equipment.

With any microform collection, there will be a need for one or more reader/printers. Some libraries report having coin-operated reader/printers for public use, but others have experienced too many maintenance problems with this arrangement. My experience has been that these pieces of equipment are too delicate and sensitive to allow general public use of them. Maintenance costs are lower and hard copy quality is better when reader/printers are operated by trained staff.

A third kind or type of equipment should be available in a microform area. Just as preventive maintenance on your home or automobile pays dividends, so will the purchase and systematic use of a film cleaning machine be a wise investment. Its regular use will mean longer film life and, consequently, decreased cost over the long run. It will also work toward increased user satisfaction which is the fundamental goal of any collection, microform or otherwise.

The final equipment need to be mentioned is cabinets to house the microforms. Costs here are subject to decisions about types of cabinets, and to varying shipping charges, and must be determined by an individual library.

Thus far, my comments have focused on space and equipment as factors to be considered in developing a microform collection. A non-physical factor which should be considered seriously is the way in which users actually use journal literature. To be sure, there are several good studies of the use of journal literature, but most use studies have investigated the subject matter consulted, the age of journals consulted, and frequencies of individual title use. What I have in mind is of a slightly different nature and might best be described by illustration. Take, for example, the cases of the historian and the mathematician. Unless he is in the final stages of first draft manuscript preparation, the historian, typically, will spend enough time with a journal article to read it thoroughly and carefully. This may require a half hour or more. The mathematician, on the other hand, leaves his desk, pencil, and paper for quick consultation of a theorem, proposition, or lemma, and will spend less time, per consultation, and over a large number of uses, with journal literature. This comparison is crude, oversimplified, and speaks about something which should be researched more than it has been, but it does suggest a consideration in deciding which journals a library should retain in paper copy and which it should convert to microforms. Similar comments may be made about the engineer, the chemist, or the physicist. Notice that the subject matter mentioned in making this point corresponds roughly with that subject matter in many branch libraries. This is because the user behavior for which I am suggesting further investigation is one of the determinants in establishing branches.

Constraints of time do not allow for anything even approaching a thorough discussion of user behavior as a factor to be considered in developing a microform collection; I will just leave with you the idea that its careful consideration is a variable which will determine user satisfaction.

Among the resources available to any library, the most important is people, so it is with staffing that I will begin my comments on the management of microform journal collections. Because the physical configuration of a library building plays a part in the staffing of service stations, and because the microform collection at Memphis State University contains a large amount of material which is not journal literature, it is located organizationally as part of the Reference Department. Three staff members are permanently assigned to the microforms room, and several other reference staff are assigned to work several hours there each week. All of these personnel have responsibilities for providing users with microforms from a secured area, for assisting them with placement of film and fiche on readers, and for making copies on the reader/printers as requested. The three staff permanently assigned to the area are all knowledgeable about the collection, and at least one is on duty each day Monday through Friday from 8 a.m. until 10 p.m. Student assistants also work in the area to aid the full-time staff. Our experience has been that this staffing pattern allows for a good response to users.

In addition to the duties already mentioned, the microforms staff routinely cleans the reader lenses on a daily basis and completes a film cleaning once each semester. Again, this is preventive maintenance and it pays long-term dividends.

A few moments ago, I mentioned the retrieval of film and fiche from a secured area. Actually, this secured area is merely a clustering of cabinets in the microform area such that they are behind a service desk which is located, along with shelving, so that the cabinets are inaccessible by the public. There are additional staff costs with this arrangement as opposed to an open area where users might find film for themselves, but these latter conditions lend themselves to misplaced, lost, or, occasionally, mutilated film. (*Playboy* on color film, issues of *Sports Illustrated*, and a few other popular magazines seem to disappear or have frames cut from them.) Fiche are especially susceptible to loss or theft and misfiling. The question of a closed versus an open microform collection is one which can be debated, but experiential evidence clearly favors the closed system.

The process of replacing paper bibliographic volumes with microfilm copy introduces certain requirements, some of which are peculiar to a particular library. Just as the physical configuration of a library building determines, in part, staff deployment, so does it dictate ceratin staff expenditures of time and effort in the establishment and management of a microform collection. In the particular library I represent, non-periodical serials are acquired, processed, and routed to various locations by the Acquisitions Department. The Periodicals Department is responsible only for journals and newspapers, and is physically located two floors removed from the microform room. In a public area immediately adjacent to the Periodicals Department is a holdings file for periodicals which, in addition to holdings information, provides location tags. Because of the physical distance between the Periodicals Department and the microforms room, there is, in the microforms room, a journal and newspaper holdings file for microforms there. This is a duplication of effort and expenditure, but it adds significantly to user acceptance of our microforms collection.

Costs and Economies

I promised earlier to avoid discussion of precise costs associated with the establishment and management of a microform journal and newspaper collection, and I will not depart from this position. I will list and comment briefly, however, on those variables, in addition to those already mentioned, which must be considered in terms of expenditures or savings.

Among the various costs and economies to which it would seem that prime consideration would be given is space, since the storage of microforms requires 90 to 98 per cent less space than that required to store paper copy. Consideration of space as an economy, however, is complicated by considerations of a local nature.[4] Many libraries do not include the use of space, along with required maintenance of that space, and the cost of utilities to heat, cool, and light it, in the annual cost of operations. Further, space costs vary from one geographical location to another. Also, the annual cost of using library space will vary as a function of the quality of the space in question.

Another difficulty in generalizing about microforms versus paper copy arises when attention is focused on the problem of mutilation of journals and the attendant costs of replacing missing pages with some form of photocopy. The microform versus paper copy differential is difficult to identify because most libraries experience the cost of replacing missing pages only after the missing pages are reported by users. Until this is done, any unreported or unknown missing pages are not known costs, but are potential costs in the sense that they may become known or reported at any time. This, however, given other considerations, speaks in favor of the view that the purchase of microforms is advantageous when note is taken of the much greater security arrangements that can be achieved with microforms.

Consideration of binding costs versus those of purchasing microfilm must recognize that the decision to bind loose issues, aside from the costs of missing issues required to complete a bibliographic volume, entails only one subscription cost. The purchase of microfilm at the end of a volume year, however, means that the library has paid for a subscription to paper copy, and then pays again for the same material in microformat. Actual costs on a title-by-title basis, and in an individual library, can be made, but it will generally be found that the purchase of microforms will be less expensive when binding charges and the overhead personnel costs associated with the binding of journals are eliminated. Our experience at Memphis State has been that it is not worth the effort required to send unbound issues of journals replaced with microfilm to back-file vendors for credit. Rather, we achieve some measure of public relations value by giving these, annually, to teaching faculty for their office and classroom use.

Space savings, the elimination of binding costs, and the elimination of costs associated with mutilation have been offered as economies. If, in fact, they are in a particular library, any savings must be applied to the added cost, when adopting a microforms program, of reading equipment, film cabinet costs, the cost of one or more reader/printers, and the cost of cleaning equipment. Further, any additional personnel costs resulting from the establishment of a microform journal and newspaper collection must be taken into account.

In my opening remarks, I made a disclaimer by saying that I had no panacea to offer to you, and that I would not try to persuade you that it would be, for your libraries, less expensive to replace journals and newspapers with microform instead of retaining the paper copy. There are too many variable factors associated with such a decision, and these factors must be considered in light of circumstances within an individual library. Rather, I have tried to describe, however briefly, a program within an individual library where circumstances have directed it toward developing a very large, but very manageable, microforms collection. As a closing comment, I will disclaim part of my earlier disclaimer and suggest that it would be cost effective in most libraries to adopt, or to accelerate, a program of replacing last year's unbound journals with microform.

References

1. Carl M. Spaulding, "Getting the Most Out of Microforms," in Louisiana State University, *Library Lectures, Numbers 29 through 35* (Baton Rouge: LSU Library): 44.

2. Charles Smith, *Micrographics Handbook* (N.P.: ARTECH House, 1978): 11.

3. Susan K. Nutter, "Microforms and the User: Key Variables of User Acceptance in a Library Environment," *Drexel Library Quarterly* 11 (October, 1975): 18.

4. William Saffady, *Micrographics* (Littleton, CO: Libraries Unlimited, 1978): 16.

STRATEGIES AND ALTERNATIVES
IN DEALING WITH THE
SERIALS MANAGEMENT BUDGET

Herbert S. White

Under a series of grants from the National Science Foundation, the Indiana University Research Center for Library and Information Science has been studying the economic interaction of libraries and the publishers of scholarly materials, and the strategies devised by libraries in dealing with what we all now know is a shortage of adequate funding. Actually, I am not sure that libraries are ever assuaged by the funds which they receive. Perhaps based on some variation of Parkinson's Law, our needs can always be adjusted to stay one step ahead of our resources, regardless of what those resources are. There are always things we have not bought, and even if we had bought them all there is no reason not to buy a second copy.

Our studies, while begun in 1973, track data back to 1969. The year 1969 is a significant one, because it probably represents the last year of "good" library funding. At the time we did not necessarily think it was all that adequate. However, what had happened since then has made us realize how good the 1960s really were. Our studies cover in total, at least for academic libraries, the ten year period starting in 1969. Although we did not consistently ask the same questions, we elicited a sufficiently common thread of information to permit the development of a clear track of emerging and changing strategies. These findings have been reported in a series of articles in the library literature[1,2] and will therefore not be reported here. However, this really provides the first opportunity to tie all our findings into one total continuum.

Changes in prices for library publications[3,4,5] have also been sufficiently reported in various publications for me not to have to dwell on this topic, any more than on the topic of whether the library budget has kept pace with the cost of library materials. It clearly has not. More significantly, it is reasonable to expect that it probably will not again, at least in the foreseeable future. Prices of serials are far easier, and far more interesting, to track than prices of books. The price of new books published varies widely from year to year, because each group of new monographs establishes an entirely new base, totally independent of what happened last year. We not only do not know what monographs will be newly published, but we also do not know in what fields they will appear, what format they will take, and whether they will be cheap or expensive. That is, we know they will be more expensive than if they had been published in the previous year, but the point is that they were not published in the previous year, and it is reasonable to assume that even in 1981 a 300-page book will, on the average, cost less than a 600-page book did in 1980. For this reason we find wild fluctuations in "average" prices, and in some fields these actually go down from one year to the next. The monographic publications field also has another character-istic which makes it far more sensitive to economic pressures than the serials field. In monographic publication the publisher is taking a risk – he is spending his money at the front end, and creating an in-ventory which may or may not sell. He has virtually no advanced orders prior to publication, and recent Supreme Court decisions make the accumulation of unsold inventory even more damaging than at present. If anything, we can therefore expect, unless Congress provides tax relief, an even greater sensitivity to library economic factors among monographic publishers. Fewer books will be pub-lished, and print runs will undoubtedly be curtailed, leading, in turn, to more out of print books.

Serials publishing, by contrast, has been almost impervious to economic pressures. Despite the fact that for some scholarly jour-nals virtually the entire publications customer market is a library market, scholarly journals continue to proliferate, apparently totally oblivious to what has been happening in libraries. I need not present any further example than the increase in library publications pub-lished by Haworth Press, in total contradiction to everything we know about library budgets and the generally perceived malaise which has seized the library profession.

There are at least two reasons for this. The first lies innately in the character of serial publication, in particular periodical (or jour-nal publication), and it concerns the phenomenon called, in business administration and accounting, cash flow. Unlike the monographic market, the serials publisher gets paid by the customer well before he spends any money at all. He can invest that money, at worst in cer-tificates of deposit at around 15%. He can adjust his publication print run to the number of subscriptions already in hand, so that there are no left-over copies cluttering up the warehouse. At worst, he can abort the publication before take-off, and he even has some options other than simply refunding the money. If he publishes more than one journal, he will try to get you to apply the purcahse price already paid to some other journal in his stable. In other words, there is very little risk in the publication of journals, and these publications tend to ignore the reality of what happens in the library budget. Our own surveys for the National Science Foundation indicated that there was a fairly large number of small not-for-profit publishers who were, by any of the rules of accounting, bankrupt. They continued to exist on cash flow, by spending next year's income on this year's expenses, and they can continue to do this as long as they do not try to stop, because they would then have to refund dollars they do not have. In fact, this very situation is partly responsible for the fact that journal titles don't get cancelled. The publisher can't afford to stop.

The other reason, perhaps even more important, is that librarians, addicted to neat and orderly systems, love serials. Not necessarily for what they contain, but for what they are. It is still, even in 1981, unthinkable for many so-called library administrators to cancel a subscription held since volume 1 after volume 5, because the absence of volume 6 negates the investment already made in the first five volumes, and we cannot afford to stop. Publishers learned a long time ago that the best way to sell monographs is to market them as part of a numbered series. If the collection contains numbers 1 through 8 and 10 through 14 of the series on electrical engineering, the pressure to try to acquire number 9, no matter what its content, becomes irresistible. This attitude, of course, is part of the residual phenomenon of the library as a scholarly collection of materials, and not as a tool to be used. It is, in academia, the faulty perception of the role of the library and it is, for many librarians, the role of the institution as well. In this environment it should not surprise anyone when I tell you that the basic strategy for dealing with the serials management budget was to avoid the problem for as long as it could possibly be avoided — basically throughout the 1970s. It is only now that we are finally starting to come to grips with this problem, and that the title of this talk even makes sense. Allow me to demonstrate, by delving back into our own survey data.

In 1969, the last of the "good" years, libraries, at least major academic libraries, subscribed by and large to any serial title which any faculty member requested or which any reasonably adventurous collection development officer could find. At least with one copy. The cancellation rate, as reported as part of our NSF study, was 0.2%. That is one in 500, and it can be argued that libraries will cancel that many just by accident or unintentionally. During the five years which followed, large academic library budgets increased at an annual rate of about 8%. We defined large academic libraries as those with periodical holdings over 5,000. That increase was not out of line with increases in the overall institutional budget for the university. However, salary budgets, for the library and probably for the university itself, increased at an annual rate of 10%. Our data did not disclose what portion of this increase was attributed to an increase in staff size and what proportion to salary improvements for continuing staff. However, in any case, that increase in the salary budget meant that, in fact, the materials budget only increased by about 5%/year. It is not likely that this shift was a conscious one. It is more likely either that salaries and materials were in fact budgeted separately, and these relationships are only accidental, or that salary increases were determined as part of some other larger strategy, and that transfers from all non-salary budgets were made to help pay for them. In fact, that is what is happening in many academic institutions at the present time. Also, it must be stressed that so-called good times and bad times are relative. We did not think the 1960s were all that great, but they were certainly an improvement of the 1970s. We may yet, in the 1980s, look back fondly and sentimentally on the 1970s, when budgets were still increasing and not decreasing.

In any case, the 5% was not nearly enough to maintain historic patterns of material acquisition in large academic libraries, which were — quite simply — to buy what people asked for and what we could find. Average price increases for periodicals varied in their impact on libraries, based on the mix of titles being purchased. In general, the more expensive scientific journals increased at a greater percentage than the lower priced humanities journals, and foreign journals, particularly from Western Europe, also increased more rapidly in price, partially because of higher rates of inflation in Western Europe (at least then), in part because of the weakening of the U.S. dollar on international exchanges. You can get different numbers from the literature depending on the mix, but our data indicate an average and perhaps conservative annual price increase for continuing periodicals of 11.2%. Conservative it may be, but it nevertheless points out a problem, because to this figure the growth in the literature itself must be added. Here again, the projections vary widely, from the 8% suggested by Anderla[6] to the flat rate projected by Gottschalk.[7] Our own estimate, done quite simply by comparisons in Ulrich's, suggests a net rate of growth (that is, new titles minus the death of old ones), of about 2%. To continue to do what they had been doing in the 1960s, libraries would have had to increase their serials budgets by an annual rate of about 13½%, out of a materials budget increase of less than half that.

Libraries did not quite achieve that rate, but they came close. What emerged was a series of strategies, not necessarily divulged or even consciously determined, to protect the continuing receipt of at least one copy of every subscription being received. This strategy, of course, has nothing to do with either use or service. It concerns the maintenance of the collection, and the *perception* of quality as seen by faculty and many librarians. Here is what occurred:

1. Libraries tended to freeze the periodicals budget where it stood, and cut down drastically on the placement of subscriptions to titles not previously owned. Libraries usually initiate subscriptions to such titles either because the periodical itself is new, or because the requirement in the community served by the library is new. In 1969, large academic libraries were adding new subscriptions at a rate of 9.4%/year. By 1973 this had almost halved, to 5.1%. Cancellation rates had more than tripled, but were still at a relatively modest 0.7%. This yields an increase in net subscriptions of 4.4%, still above most estimates of actual growth, and a clear indication that libraries were trying to protect the periodicals budget. However, where decisions were being made, they were made in favor of keeping the existing title and foregoing the new one. Comparing the decision patterns of 1969 and 1973, the determination to forego a new title which in 1969 would have been bought was made in 1973 seven times as often as the decision to cancel an existing title to make room for a new one. It is likely that faculty shared in this ranking of priorities, or agreed with it or would have agreed with it if asked. Known old favorites are hard to dispense with, and in particular newly published journals yield few clues as to their importance from citation patterns and ranking in data bases. However, when we recognize that some emerging subject disciplines are *only* covered by new journals, this conservative strategy raises some questions about its validity.

2. Libraries cancelled duplicate subscriptions. In most academic libraries the rate of duplicates is not large to start with, and rarely exceeds 5%. During the period 1969--73 better than 60% of these were cancelled. Duplicates are usually placed for one of two reasons, heavy use and branch location. Studies by Blair Stewart[8] and others,[9,10] have told us that, in confirmation of Bradford's Law, a few periodical titles are used a lot and a lot of titles are used very little. In cancelling duplicates, libraries were therefore favoring collection integrity over service needs, and undoubtedly favoring faculty interests over student interests.

3. Libraries also cancelled foreign titles for two reasons. First, these titles were expensive and getting more expensive. Secondly, American scholars, unlike their European and Asiatic counterparts, are frequently unilingual. I could cite studies from my own NASA days which clearly indicate that when Americans cannot read it in English, they do not read it at all. This may be deplorable, but it is true. Curiously, in cancelling foreign titles libraries frequently

cancelled the titles it might be more difficult to obtain in the future if really needed. They did this, perhaps in contradiction to the collection development urge, because they felt instinctively that this material was little used and that they would not have to borrow it anyway. Libraries did this instinctively because few used any hard data, or had any hard data available. It turns out that their instincts are pretty good. Our latest study indicates that titles cancelled by academic libraries are rarely if ever borrowed after cancellation.

4. As I have already begun to indicate, libraries did not, and to a large extent still do not, make cancellation decisions based on availability from other sources. The concept of a consortium decision which assigns responsibility for purchase and allows protected cancellation, so feared by publishers, is beginning to emerge but is still in its very early stages. In 1973–75 it did not exist at all. Libraries were and to some extent still are too competitive for that. The fact that library A across the state has a title is not a reason for cancellation, it is a reason for subscription to keep up.

5. Fifth, and finally, despite assertions by librarians and fears by publishers, libraries did not cancel because of price. If they did it was only because a title already on the "hit" list was pushed over the brim by its high price. When libraries cancelled, they cancelled because of value or perceived lack of value. Publisher friends have told me that price increases, which make a substantial difference in individual renewals and cancellation, have absolutely no impact on library renewals. Libraries do what they think they must, and there is clear evidence of titles which did not increase in price being cancelled to clear funds to maintain crucial titles which did. Or, as Eugene Garfield, president of the Institute for Scientific Information, once put it: "Every time Chemical Abstracts increases its price, libraries cancel the Science Citation Index." The average price of cancelled journals in large academic libraries was lower than the average price of retained journals.

How then, in large part, did libraries cope with the insatiable appetite of the serials budget? By feeding that budget, through transfers from the monographic budget. In 1969 academic libraries were spending $2.00 on books for every dollar spent on serials. By 1973 this ratio had shifted, with $1.16 spent on books for every dollar spent on serials. By 1976 the line had been clearly crossed, and libraries were spending $1.23 on serials for every dollar spent on books. Actually, the impact is even greater than that, because some libraries were changing the definition of what was a serial and what was a monograph, shifting monographic serial titles into the monographic budget to retain the ability to review on an annual basis. However, even without this additional shift, the results were dramatic enough. Let me demonstrate with a small example. If, in 1969, the library had a unit of $3.00 of which it spent $2.00 on books and $1.00 on serials, by 1976 that $3.00 had grown, through an annual growth rate of 5%, to $4.22. Of that $4.22, the library was now spending $1.89 on books, and $2.33 on serials. In other words, the monographic budget has declined, in actual dollars and not just in inflated ones, from $2.00 to $1.89. We don't really know what that means in a loss of purchasing power, because price increases for monographs are so dependent on subject mix. However, if you care to assume a 10% annual increase (still considerably less than for periodicals), then $2.00 in 1969 would have had to be $3.90 to maintain a constant acquisitions rate, and libraries were therefore buying less than half the books in 1976 that they bought in 1969. By contrast, the growth in serials expenditures from $1.00 in 1969 to $2.33 in 1976 provided an annual rate of growth of almost 13%, or just about the inflationary price increases. Up to 1976, academic libraries were managing the serials budget, and I would have to use managing in quotes, by transferring into it whatever it needed to maintain its present patterns. There are two comments I always have to make at this point. I am invariably confronted after my talks by an angry academic library administrator, who tells me that his or her library was making tough decisions way back in 1972. I do not doubt it or deny it. These are averages, and I am sure that there were administrators who managed and evaluated their serials budgets way back then. It's just that most libraries did not.

Secondly, every time I divulged these shifts between 1973 and 1976 librarians hastened to assure me that these aberrations were temporary, that the transfer of funds from the monographic to the serials budget had now stopped, because it just had to. Well, it has not. It has slowed, but it has not stopped. The reason is not difficult to determine, and it gets right back to the emphasis on collection integrity and on the visibility of change. The cancellation of a subscription is a conscious and a highly visible action. The change is real and it is painful. A cut in the monographic budget, by contrast, is really quite vague. We are impacting the purchase of books next year, and we do not even yet know what books they are. In fact, as a faculty member, as long as you buy the specific books I ask you to buy (there usually are not too many) the cut in the monographic budget has no meaning for me whatsoever. Never forget that when faculty members talk about the library, they mean their own personal and particular collection. They have no objection to your buying other things, but they are not going to lose any sleep over it, either.

Of course, this shift from the monographic to the serials budget impacts some disciplines more than others. The physical sciences, in general, are strongly dependent on the periodical literature. The humanities, on the other hand, are far more oriented to monographs. Where shifts have taken place across departmental disciplines, there has been a shift in emphasis. There is nothing necessarily wrong with this, as long as it is being done consciously. It could be argued that historically libraries have over-emphasized humanities at the expense of the sciences, in part because librarians themselves tended to be humanists and bought the things they knew. Most libraries, however, particularly large academic libraries, tend to freeze allocation relationships between departments. This practice may not be good management (whatever inequities historically exist become perpetuated), but it is good, or at least survival, politics. However, what this has done, particularly within the physical sciences, is to focus on the needs of the serials budget at the expense of the monographic budget. I know of schools which, with departmental allocations, have stopped buying monographs in certain fields and are spending 100 cents of every dollar on serials. This decision must be seen by any conscientious library administrator as disastrous and foolhardy and it would seem to me one of the responsibilities of the library administrator, if the administrator is truly responsible for *administering*, not to allow this to happen, even if it is what the faculty, in their ignorance (and they really know far less about the material in their fields than they pretend to), prefer to do.

Since 1976, it is clear that libraries have run out of options to avoid serials cancellations, and they are now cancelling not just subscriptions, but sole and last remaining copies. Our most recent survey[11] was designed to determine how this process was being carried forward. In part, we know, or at least have reason to suspect, that academic funding and library funding in the 1980s is not going to provide any alleviation to this problem. In part we also wanted to know whether publishers were correct in their suspicion and fear that photocopying, interlibrary loan, and consortia were playing a large role in shaping library cancellation decisions. In undertaking this survey, we decided to try to avoid a problem which we had encountered earlier, in the fact that the actions which libraries reported as a management policy tended to contradict what we saw as a specific action. There was and perhaps still is a good deal of wishful thinking about the exact and tough scientific management process in the library. We decided, instead, to ask libraries about specific decisions with regard to specific titles -- both new subscriptions and cancellations -- which we obtained from the publishers. For this title -- why did you do what you did?

Very quickly, with regard to new subscriptions, and there are still new subscriptions in major academic libraries, there is virtually no evaluation taking place. Libraries buy what they perceive they should, or what they perceive they must. Libraries buying new subscriptions are not part of an overall strategy, they are a specific action in response to a specific request, because somebody suggested, requested, or demanded that it do so. In making this determination the relative ranking process, which is frequently used to determine what will be renewed and what is cancelled in times of shrinking budgets, is usually not brought into play. The decision can occur any time during the year, although the journal could very well be ranked at the time of renewal. The process of new subscriptions is then largely a political process. Better than 26% are reinstatements of subscriptions previously cancelled — not because there is now more money — but because faculty pressure has increased. In some cases it comes simply from one new individual who has joined the user group and wants it.

Libraries do not buy titles because they just learned about them. The suggestion that interlibrary loan is good for publishers because libraries find out about titles they then purchase simply has no supporting evidence. From 296 responses, not a single one suggested, even as part of multiple factors, that the library had learned about this wonderful title by borrowing it. Similarly, the disclosure of a new and promising title through citations, literature references and abstracting tools or data bases accounts for only about 8% of the subscriptions. Borrowing the title frequently might appear to be a good reason for subscribing, but it only pertains in 6.4% of the cases. A group of collection development specialists once told me that as budgets tighten, fewer decisions are made, because there are things the library must do politically, and when that is all the money available, that's all that happens. I didn't really believe it then, but I certainly do now. Subscribing because of an assigned responsibility from a network or consortium accounts for less than 1%. That figure is low, but it may just be a start. It will have to be watched. Cancellations follow a different pattern. First of all, libraries don't even consider cancellation unless forced to by budgetary stringency. That may seem obvious, but it shouldn't. Operations research tells us that it is more difficult to find things in a larger collection than a smaller one. In other words, materials never used should presumably be cancelled even if you have the money because they inhibit the use of material which is used. It never happens that way.

Although many libraries have attemted to shift the burden of cancellation decision to the user (a questionable evaluative though certainly protective tactic), our data clearly show that cancellation decisions are most frequently made unilaterally by the library staff. Users, who like to give advice concerning what to buy, are more difficult to find in making decisions to cancel.

The overwhelming reason for cancelling a subscription is the perception that the material is little used, and we can get away with cancelling it. This decision is infrequently based on use data, or on determination of coverage in indexes and data bases. These decisions account for less than 3% of the reasons. It is not because of price, which is listed as a factor, even allowing for multiple responses, in less than 9% of the responses.

Libraries are now cancelling sole subscriptions in the collection, 82% were the only copies in the collection. While 18% were still duplicate or branch copies, that number is much smaller than the cancellation breakdown of the early 1970s. Of course, it is possible and perhaps probable that the easily identifiable cancellations are already gone.

Only 15% of the respondents planned any sort of formal review to determine whether the cancellation decision was in fact valid. It may be that these libraries found the cancellation a painful enough process without wanting to reopen it. It may also be that they know, as indicated by our data, that if the cancellation was a mistake somebody, usually an irate user, will tell them.

Was this cancellation, arrived at so subjectively and without hard data, a mistake? In most cases it would appear that these instinctive judgments are in fact correct, and libraries are cancelling those titles which minimally impact service response. Of course, if you value the collection in and of itself without considering the question of use, that is another matter. Only a little better than 3% of the respondents reported the need to borrow the title at least once in a year period since cancellation. This may be just as well, because two-thirds of the cancelling libraries did not even consider the question of availability on interlibrary loan as part of the cancellation decision. They either assumed that it could be borrowed if needed, or they were confident that nobody would want it, anyway.

Ninety-two percent of the respondents indicated that the decision to cancel was an independent decision, made without consideration of network or consortium membership or availability. The fact that 8% did take this into some sort of consideration is surprising, not because the percentage is large, but because it appears for the very first time in any of our studies. If, indeed, this percentage grows rapidly in the 1980s, then publishers may have grounds for their fears that library cooperation may become a systematic approach to the subscription and cancellation decision. At this point the emphasis should not be overplayed. Only 2% of the cancellations were based on the specific knowledge or assurance that somebody else had the title, the others just assumed it.

Conclusions and Projections

What conclusions and emerging strategies present themselves? First, let me make a confession. I have been using the words serials and periodicals interchangeably, because it turns out that in allocating and controlling their budgets libraries cannot differentiate between periodicals and non-periodical serials. However, we do know that the great bulk of the serials budget goes for periodicals, and from this point on I am talking about periodicals.

It doesn't take a great sage to forecast that things aren't going to get better. Library funding for materials may or may not improve, but is is not going to increase at a rate to keep pace with the cost of materials and with the growth in materials. As I have pointed out, serials, unlike monographs, are almost impervious to the economic roller-coaster. And that roller-coaster points down, for perhaps the next decade but not because anyone dislikes libraries. Everyone still loves them. It is because of a fundamental shift away from big government which I suspect is here to stay at least for a while, and because of a decline in higher education brought about by the change in the birth rate. We have known this change was coming for the last 18 years, we just have not done much about it.

Library funds for materials will not keep pace. In fact, I would be very worried if they did keep pace, because any extraordinary effort to continue to support the library collection will inevitably come at the expense of the library staff and library services, and then we will really become the warehouse that many faculty think we are anyway. It behooves us, then, to cut prudently and on our own initiative, and to begin to cut before we are forced to, although there is no evidence to date of such actions. Where do we cut? I think the evidence is quite clear that, in order to protect the serials, or periodicals, budget, we have already done great harm to the monographic budget, unless somebody wants to suggest that we have been squandering funds in that area in the 1950s and 1960s. These cuts must come in our periodicals subscriptions, and they will probably be deep and continuing cuts. Hopefully, unless we want to turn our backs completely on our service responsibilities, they will not simply involve whatever duplicates remain. They will be single subscriptions, and we will have to choose them. It is not likely that our clientele will willingly choose them for us, and if they do they probably will not choose the right ones.

Which ones do we pick? To answer that question we must first look at two fundamental uses of periodicals. Some are used extensively, some even exclusively, for browsing and for current access. These titles must be retained. There is little point in trying to borrow on inter-library loan the latest issue of "Nature," or of "Barron's."

Fortunately, there aren't too many of these. Many if not most of the remaining titles are required in response to retrospective research — by checking bibliographies, by accessing data bases, by surveys of the literature. They are not used by students, except perhaps doctoral students. They are used by faculty. Access requirements to these titles are not immediate, and we can satisfy our users if, and it is a very big if, we can assure delivery within 48 hours. I have been conducting a little survey among my friends who are fellow faculty members and fellow library users, and I have yet to get a negative response to the question: "If I deliver these items to you, without fail, within 48 hours, do you care where they come from?"

Fortunately, for us, such access delivery systems for periodicals are indeed possible, because the average periodical request, from ISI's OATS service data, is less than 20 pages, and such articles rarely exceed 50 pages. Delivery service for monographs is far more difficult because of their length and is of course another reason for reversing the emphasis on serials collections as an in-house resource at the expense of monographs.

I think that we can identify those titles in the periodicals collection which must be accessible on demand, and those which can be handled as an allocated responsibility under a resource sharing system. This determination is, of course, precisely what publishers have been fearing, and also exactly what our latest survey sought to measure. A start is being made, albeit a tiny one.

To accomplish this, we must first of all stop measuring and evaluating the library in terms of the size of its collection. The Clapp-Jordan formula and the rankings published by ARL have always been something of a joke in their attempts to define the relative quality of the library, but they become a menace to effective resource sharing. Secondly, we must improve both bibliographic access and document delivery to provide that 48-hour service I have been talking about. The bibliographic access system, through terminals, is just about in place. The document delivery system is still nowhere near in place, because we depend on two fundamentals, one a disaster, the other a myth. The disaster is the postal system; the myth that interlibrary loan is a self-evident good that all libraries willingly share, because we all benefit from it. There has been an underlying assumption that everyone favors interlibrary loan because lending and borrowing cancel each other out, and therefore the economics do not have to be exact. We know, from our studies and others, that this is nonsense. There are borrowers and there are lenders, and to expect lending institutions to underwrite the poverty of borrowers is not only unfair, it is unconscionable as a management policy for librarians who should be allocating their scarce resources to serve their own clientele. Of course you can solve all this with a national system, underwritten by Uncle Sam, which will supply everything free of charge — that is, free to everyone except the taxpayer. I doubt that this is likely to happen, and I would even have the temerity to suggest it should not happen. If regional resource sharing, with small duplicated local collections and large readily available regional ones, have any validity at all, then the cost of the system and the transactions should be recoverable from the savings at each local library. Interlibrary lending will work when it is in the interests (and I mean financial interests) of the lender to do so. Give them a little extra surplus on top of costs and they'll even compete for the privilege of lending, by promising faster response time. Of course, when we talk about lending, we don't mean lending of the document at all. We mean photocopying. In virtually every case, from our NSF surveys, a copy of the article was made. It was either made by the lender who, after all, does not want to ship the bound volume out of the state. Where, because of the lack of adequate copying equipment, the lender did in fact transmit the original, the borrower almost inevitably made a copy before returning it.

We cannot depend on the post office for 48-hour delivery, but we do not need to. Most of Europe, recognizing that the traditional mail system is just one alternative in a continually changing and emerging spectrum, has put information transfer technology development under the control of the postal authorities. Here, we have done it differently, but we have the technology to transfer pages via telephone lines and via satellites for many years. We just have not used it for library processes, although it will work acceptably for just about any quality except art reproductions or medical photographs. The economics have not been too attractive, but the economics are improving, and we have not a clue as to what the present independent fiefdom approach costs this nation. The technology is certainly improving — almost daily. In any case, we could start, on a regional basis, with station wagons on a shuttle schedule, or with graduate students who drive the 100 miles between campuses once every two days to pick up and deliver.

Will such a serious change, the development of conscious resource sharing and the purchasing within the library community of fewer copies, have an impact on scholarly publishing? Undoubtedly, but I do not know what that impact is, and while I care as a citizen, I am not sure it is my responsibility to care as a librarian. I would agree with De Gennaro[12] that it is not our responsibility to ensure the survival of scholarly publishing. Scholarly publishing, particularly with regard to serials, has, as already demonstrated, a resilience of its own. It seems to me that the real answer is to consider scholarly publishing a logical extension of the education process. It seems ludicrous that government, at all levels, subsidizes and supports education from kindergarten to school lunch programs to scholarships to research grants and laboratory equipment, and after spending 20 years to get an individual to the point where he or she finally produces something useful, then decides it has no interest in seeing that anyone else finds out about the results of all that investment.

It has also been suggested that, instead of saving money, such a tactic will only increase the price of individual subscriptions, and left to itself, it will. Publishers know full well, and our studies confirm it, that libraries have no price resistance. They pay what it costs, while individual subscribers will cancel if the price gets high. That is the fundamental reason behind differential pricing, and it makes sense. If the price really gets outrageous, then the entire consortium can decide to cancel, and tell its scholarly users why. If that happens, we may really have the death of some scholarly journals, but it won't be your fault. Paradoxically enough, individual publishers do not really worry about it either, they all think it will affect journals but not their own. Don't worry about it, it isn't your problem.

Is it legal? I do not know, but since it makes sense and can develop overwhelming popular support, it either already is or Congress can and will make it so. Our system of laws adapts to reality. We have adapted to the reality of photocopying by stretching the concept of "fair use" in judicial opinions and finally incorporating it in the new copyright law. If you do not believe that the legal system will protect the virtue and public good of education, research, and scholarship, read the court opinions of the Williams and Wilkins case, in which the publisher sued the National Library of Medicine for copyright infringement. All the law is on the side of the minority opinion, which supported the publisher. However, the majority found for the government, with the pious hope that Congress would clear up the confusion, because no Court was willing to say that publishers must be paid, and medical research be damned — let them all die of cancer. And, of course, Congress has not cleared up the confusion in the most recent law, and it will not in any future efforts either. It is time for us, as library administrators, to take some initiative and some responsibility for our policies and directions. Our own NSF studies show that, between 1969 and almost the present, librarians have wavered and vacillated, have temporized and followed expediency — and have done almost everything imaginable to avoid confronting faculty and administrators with the new reality — that it is not a matter of your not loving us enough and giving us enough money — that it represents a fundamental change in library service — that the concept of the Alexandrian stand-alone resource is dead. We can refuse to face that, and watch both resources and services as measured in traditional concepts atrophy and wither, or we can apply what we know about collection use and what we can learn

40

about information transfer mechanisms to develop a new and dynamic system — completely different but probably at least as good.

NOTES

1. White, Herbert S. "Publishers, Libraries and Costs of Journal Subscriptions in Times of Funding Retrenchment," *Library Quarterly* 46(October 1976):359–377.

2. White, Herbert S. "The Economic Interaction of Scholarly Journal Publishing and Libraries During the Present Period of Cost Increases and Budget Reductions: Implications for Serials Librarians," *Serials Librarian* 1(Spring 1977):221--230.

3. Brown, Norman B. and Jane Phillips. "Price Indexes for 1980. U.S. Periodicals and Serials Services," *Library Journal* 105(July 1980):1486--1491.

4. Grannis, Chandler B. "Book Title Output and Average Prices 1978--79," in *Bowker Annual of Library and Book Trade Information 1980*, New York, Bowker, 1980, p446--453.

5. Williams, Sally F. "Price of U.S. and Foreign Published Materials," in *Bowker Annual of Library and Book Trade Information 1980*, New York, Bowker, 1980, p454–466.

6. Aderla, J. Georges. "The Growth of Scientific and Technical Information — A Challenge," *Information* part 2--3, no. 3 (1974):1–52.

7. Gottschalk, Charles M. and Winifred F. Desmond. "Worldwide Census of Scientific and Technical Serials," *American Documentation* 14(July 1963):188--194.

8. Stewart, Blair. "Periodicals and the Liberal Arts College Library," *College and Research Libraries* 36(September 1975): 371–378.

9. Trueswell, Richard W. "Growing Libraries: Who Needs Them? A Statistical Basis for the No-Growth Collection," in *Farewell to Alexandria*, ed. by Daniel Gore, Westport, CT, Greenwood, 1976.

10. Kent, Allen and others. *Use of Library Materials: The University of Pittsburgh Study*. Library and Information Science

Series, vol. 26. New York, Marcel Dekker, 1979.

11. White, Herbert S. "Factors in the Decision by Individuals and Libraries to Place or Cancel Subscriptions to Scholarly and Research Journals," *Library Quarterly* 50(July 1980):287–309.

12. De Gennaro, Richard. "Escalating Journal Prices: Time to Fight Back," *American Libraries* 8(February 1977):69–74.

SERIALS DESELECTION:
A DREADFUL DILEMMA

Roger K. Hanson

In recent years many libraries, especially academic libraries, have had to make difficult decisions regarding the most effective use of the library's acquisitions budget. For many it is a dreadful dilemma. Since these words are included in the title of this paper, perhaps they should be defined and put in their proper context. The words "serial" and "deselection" should also be defined. A serial is defined as any publication appearing in parts, usually with no termination planned or expected. Thus serials include periodicals and continuations in some libraries. Too frequently the terms serials and periodicals are used interchangeably and, therefore, it is difficult to do a comparative analysis from one institution to another. In looking at compilations of library statistical data this variance becomes apparent. In one statistical compilation there is one institution spending $2,000 more than another yet reporting about 7,500 fewer current serial subscriptions. One institution is receiving only 400 more current serials than another but spending $250,000 more for current serial expenditures.

A dictionary definition of the word "deselect" is "to dismiss from a training program." This is probably an apt definition to use since serials are certainly an important part of any academic training program. Deselection should probably not be confused with weeding. Weeding is often understood to mean the process of removing unneeded, obsolete or duplicate materials from library collections. A dictionary definition is "to remove the less desirable portions." In the case of serials deselection this may very well not be the case.

Webster's Dictionary defines the word "dreadful" as "extremely distasteful, unpleasant or shocking." Another definition is "causing great or oppressive fear." Possibly each of these definitions applies to serials deselection. The word "dilemma" is defined as "a problem seemingly incapable of a satisfactory solution." At the outset of the deselection process, this may very likely be everyone's mindset; but faced with the realities of the situation you realize you must proceed and, hopefully, make the best decisions along the way.

The process of canceling journal subscriptions can be very time consuming and complex. A cursory review of library literature does not reveal any standardized procedures to follow. This is understandable since no two institutions are identical; however, there may be common steps in the process and some common factors to consider regardless of size or purpose of the library involved with the process. This paper will identify the steps followed by one institution and factors used to determine titles for cancellation. An article written by Jeffrey Broude[1] revealed that many of the same factors were considered in a similar process at California State University at Dominquez Hills. It should be stressed, however, that in both cases the great amount of faculty involvement was a key to successful completion of the project.

There are many steps in the serial cancellation process before final decisions are made. Final decisions are only the conclusions of some process. According to Stephen M. Archer[2] the process includes: (1) The activities of discovering and defining things to decide about; (2) determining the objectives of the organization; (3) the enumeration and preparation of the alternative ways of making a decision. I would suggest the following steps and procedures in not only making the decision to cancel serials but how to do it, and planning for its effects on the future.

1. What are the reasons for having to make the decision in the first place? Chart the past history of the acquisitions budget and how it has been affected by annual appropriations, inflation, increased enrollments, changes in educational programs and probably several others. This past history is important to everyone involved with the process, and rest assured the questions will be asked by institutional administrators. Be prepared to justify the entire library budget.

2. When the historical analysis has been completed it is time to decide what the options are, then select the option (or options) that will have the least damaging long-term effect.

3. Assuming the decision made in the second step of the process is to cancel serial subscriptions, then identify the factors to consider in the deselection process and the procedure to follow.

4. After serial subscriptions have been cancelled there are still several decisions to make. Among those to be considered are: (1) What should be done with the existing backrun of the title? (2) Do the cancellations have any effect on space needs? (3) If plans are to reinstate the journal at a later time, how should the library fill the gap created between the cancellation and the reinstatement (bound volumes, microfilm, etc.)?

5. Planning for the future. If, after compiling the historical data in Step 1 and further studies that may be completed, the library feels that the acquisitions budget is inadequate to support the educational and research objectives of the institution, develop a strategy to seek an increased level of funding.

The University of Utah had been dealing with a continuing problem of annual budgetary increases not keeping pace with inflation for a period of several years. During this time period, however, the library did receive two very substantial contributions for the purchase of library materials. In 1968, Mr. J. Willard Marriott made a gift of $1,000,000 which greatly enhanced the strength of the library by allowing it to purchase several of the missing backruns of journals, fill gaps in monographic collections and most significantly, to strengthen Special Collections. In 1974, University President, David P. Gardner designated that $500,000 from the President's Club Fund Drive be used for strengthening library collections. While both of these contributions greatly strengthened the library, few people realized that they had little or no impact on serial subscriptions; therefore, when the decision to cancel serial subscriptions was announced, the reasons for it may not have been as clearly understood and accepted as perhaps they should have been. As Robert P. Holley,[3] Assistant Director for Technical Services at the University of Utah, stated in his report on serial cancellations, "A library using 'soft' money to maintain serial subscriptions with their accompanying long-term commitment would be the equivalent of a university hiring tenured faculty with 'soft' money." The ultimate reason that led to the decision to cancel subscriptions was a 4% reduction in the University of Utah's budget base effective July 1, 1980. It should be made clear that the University's budget for the 1980--81 fiscal year was not 4% less than the previous year. The 4% reduction was implemented before applying the increased appropriations from the Legislature to the 1980–81 budget. This procedure made a significant difference on the decision-making process. The end result after applying the 4% reduction to the 1979-80 budget and the increases to the 1980–81 budget was a 1.0% net increase in the acquisitions budget. The difference is that, in making the reductions before the increased appropriations, you must reduce existing programs rather than being able to apply the reduced percentage increase across the board. Theoretically, the 4% reduction to the base budget could have been applied across the board as well, but whether or not this is a sound administrative practice should be seriously questioned.

As its contribution to the University's 4% reduction the Marriott Library at the University of Utah made the following recommendations, in priority order, to decrease the Library's budget:

PROPOSED
LIBRARY PROGRAM REDUCTIONS

Priority	Program	Savings
1.	Elimination of Branch Library Service	$40,000
2.	Elimination of Library Administrative Personnel	25,000
3.	Reduction in Program to Convert Serial Backruns to Microfilm	6,000
4.	Reduction in Cataloging Reference Collection	5,000
5.	Reduction in Service to Microform Patrons	8,000
6.	Elimination of One (1) FTE and Reduction of Hourly Assistance in Cataloging	13,750
7.	Reduction in Monograph & Serial Acquisitions	60,000
8.	Reduction in Hours of Service in Special Collections and in Processing Manuscripts	13,500
9.	Reduction of Secretarial Support for Public Services by .5 FTE	4,350
10.	Elimination of Two (2) FTE Staff Positions in Administration	19,680
11.	Reduction in Technical Services Hourly Budget	5,000

$200,280

These were accepted by the University administration with only slight modification, but the need for canceling serial subscriptions was not clearly understood. In fact, it may have been viewed as being done for impact, publicity or even retaliation. It was because of this that Dr. Robert Holley prepared a clear, concise report detailing all of the factors influencing the decision. Proper credit must go to him for much of the information in this paper.

This was not the first time during the decade of the 1970s that the Marriott Library had experienced cutbacks in periodicals. In 1970–71 and 1973–74 modest reductions were made in attempts to hold expenditures at the same level as the preceding year. This fact was mentioned in the report, but 1973–74 was used as the base year for the fiscal analysis completed.

One of the major concerns of research libraries is the percentage of the acquisitions budget expended for serials. In some institutions this expenditure is getting very high and could soon consume the entire budget if increased funding does not equal or exceed inflationary costs.

The median of the total acquisition expenditures for serials in university libraries that are members of the Association of Research

46

Libraries has increased approximately 10% during the past four years as indicated by the following table.

	$	%
FY 75--76	$515,594	44.9
FY 76--77	590,745	46.0
FY 77--78	713,139	50.9
FY 78--89	825,121	53.2
FY 79--80	904,190	55.2

The number of institutions included in the median expenditure reduces the effect of extreme cases, but even so an increase of over 10% during a four-year period is a very significant shift in expenditures. The difference between the extremes and the median may be analogous to movement in a mutual fund vs. speculative stocks.

From a random selection of ten annual reports of library directors at ARL libraries, seven of them elaborate on concerns about maintaining subscriptions. In Mr. Warren Kuhn's 1978–79 annual report from Iowa State University[4] he states that at Iowa State University the expenditure for serials increased 22.8% from 1977--78 to 1978--79 and the percentage of the acquisitions budget spent on serials increased from 48.5% to 57%.

The following paragraph was taken from the 1979--80 report of Mr. Kenneth E. Toombs, Director of Libraries at the University of South Carolina.[5]

"The relatively static book budget since 1974--75 has greatly hindered the library's ability to maintain the quality in the collections and to support the University's programs adequately. During the period 1975--76 the library reduced its periodical holdings by more than 600 titles in an effort to achieve a stable book budget and since that time has been extremely careful about adding new periodical titles. However, it is obvious that additional titles must be dropped during the coming year if any funds are to be left for monographs."

In a recent telephone conversation with Mr. Toombs he reported that they are again in the process of cancelling subscriptions.

Paragraphs such as the preceding quote from Mr. Toombs and the following from Mr. Basil Stuart-Stubbs, University Librarian at the University of British Columbia, are not uncommon and are indicative of problems yet to come for many libraries.[6]

"In the current year, subscriptions are expected to cost over

$1.6 million, over $200,000 more than in 1979–80. Since any programme of cancellations requires the careful, title-by-title examination of subscription lists, in consultation with members of faculty, it is not something that can be accomplished in a fortnight. Therefore the Library had no recourse but to recommend to the Senate Library Committee that the entire increase of $250,000 be allocated to serials, and that budget items for the purchase of books be held to existing levels or reduced. In anticipation of a further shortfall in 1981–82, planning for periodical cancellations is under way."

Although the Marriott Library has not formally established the percentage of the total acquisitions budget to be spent on serials, we have great concern about erosion of buying power for monographic materials and have, therefore, arbitrarily used a figure of 60% as an upper limit for serial expenditures. We are in the process of further analysis to provide supporting data for this percentage or determine a more appropriate percentage. If convincing data can be generated, it may prove very beneficial in the future when providing justification for budgetary increases.

The graph below gives a comparison of the library acquisitions budget for monographs and serials over the past seven years.

It is interesting to note from the following table the difference in expenditures as compared to the budget we had established for serials.

SERIALS AND CSO'S AS A
PERCENT OF TOTAL ACQUISITIONS

FISCAL YEAR	BUDGET	EXPENDITURES
1973	41.3%	46.0%
1974	40.9%	49.3%
1975	45.7%	49.9%
1976	51.6%	54.7%
1977	46.5%	49.7%
1978	48.8%	53.6%
1979	53.9%	58.8%
1980	54.9%	

Although the total acquisitions budget increased only 13% in 1978, 5.1% in 1979 and 3.6% in 1980, the percentage increase from 1973 to 1979 has been 95.2%. It is understandably unclear why with such a percentage increase the library should have to cancel serials when inflation, according to the Consumer Price Index, increased by

COMPARISON OF LIBRARY ACQUISITION BUDGET
FOR MONOGRAPHS AND SERIALS

85% and the commonly used price index of U.S. periodicals from *Library Journal*[7] showed an increase of 87.4% during the same time period. The University of Utah's expenditures for serials from 1973 to 1979 increased by 148.8%. This percentage is a pretty accurate indicator of increases in subscription costs because relatively few new titles had been added; during most of this time period, departments have been required to cancel a subscription of comparable cost in order to obtain the new subscription. The increase in expenditures for serials was 16.8% in 1978 and 18.4% in 1979. When considering the total acquisitions budget increased only 13% in 1978 and 5.1% in 1979, it becomes apparent why the percentage of the total acquisitions budget spent for serials increased so rapidly; but it does not explain why the Library's expenditure for serials increased 61.4% more than the U.S. periodical price index. The explanation for this lies in the fact that the mix of periodicals at the Marriott Library is not typical of that used in arriving at the periodical price indexes.

49

The University of Utah is academically strong in the Sciences, and a fairly accurate estimate of serials expenditures indicates that 55%--65% is spent for science serials. The average price of serials in Chemistry and Physics has increased from $56.61 in 1973 to $137.45 in 1980, a 142.8% increase. In addition to having a high percentage of science journals, there is also a significant number of foreign journals. Disbursements to two of our major vendors of foreign journals (from 1978--79 to 1979–80) increased by about 34% to one vendor and 36% to the other. The devaluation of the dollar in foreign markets, coupled with inflation, has caused this increase.

The information provided on inflation in the cost of serials, the change in percentage of the acquisitions budget spent for serials, and the low percentage increases in the acquisitions budget provided convincing evidence that additional funds are required to maintain subscriptions. The natural question to follow then is what other portion of the library budget can possibly be reduced to provide additional funds for acquisitions. Since the largest portion of the total library budget is spent for personnel, be prepared to defend this portion of your budget. When comparing the expenditures for staff at the Uniersity of Utah Library to those of other comparable research libraries and measuring the student to librarian ratio, it is readily apparent that further reductions in personnel should not be made, although we did reduce staffing by 11 FTE positions with the 4% budget reduction. To help accomplish these staff reductions, we recommended closing two branch libraries, to reduce the budget for hourly employees and by not filling vacant positions. Fortunately, the reduction in force could be accomplished by attrition. Regarding the two branch libraries, the decision was made by the University Administration that if the two colleges involved wished to retain the branch libraries, they would have to reimburse the Marriott Library for the total cost of operating them. In both cases the colleges have placed a higher priority on other programs and, therefore, the branch libraries have been closed and the collections returned to the main library and integrated with other collections in the same subjects which are much stronger than the collections in the branch libraries.

As already indicated, the Marriott Library's recommendations to accomplish the 4% reduction in the base budget was accepted by the University administration with only slight modification and did include cancellation of approximately $40,000 worth of serial subscriptions. The next decision then was how to proceed.

By the time the decision was made to cancel serial subscriptions, sufficient information had been distributed through normal communication channels, e.g., the Council of Academic Deans, the Marriott Library *Newsletter*, and faculty contact through the department's library representatives, so the question was not "why," but "how." The decision was made by the Library Administration that the library staff must provide the leadership and do most of the work to accomplish the objective, but there must also be faculty input throughout the process. I cannot stress enough the importance of faculty involvement. The Library's Acquisitions Committee, chaired by the Assistant Director for Technical Services, was charged with the responsibility of implementing the required budget adjustments. Now that the process has been completed with a minimal amount of problems or delay, perhaps the procedure they used may be recommended for use at other institutions.

The first step in the process was to establish seven deselection groups, each covering broad subject areas. The deselection groups and the subject areas/departments included in each were:

1. SCIENCE: Biology; Chemistry; Computer Science; Engineering; Mathematics; Mining; Physics.
2. SOCIAL SCIENCE: Anthropology; Sociology; and Political Science.
3. EDUCATION & GENERAL REFERENCE: Education; Educational Systems & Learning Resources; Family & Consumer Studies; General Reference; Health, Physical Education and Recreation; Library Science; and Military Science.
4. BUSINESS: Business and Economics.
5. HUMANITIES: Communications; English; History; Languages; Literature; Philosophy; Religion; Speech; and Theatre Arts.
6. FINE ARTS: Architecture; Art; Dance; and Music.
7. MIDDLE EAST.

The second step in the process was to arrive at a preliminary quota (a dollar figure) for each group. Since at the time the Library did not have hard data for serials expenditures by subject areas, the committee spent considerable time to arrive at their best judgment for each. This information was distributed and input sought in order to reach agreement for each group. As a result of this exercise, the library now assigns a broad Library of Congress classification to each title which will allow for continuous monitoring of expenditures by subject area. The amount assigned for reduction by each group was:

1.	Science	$19,000
2.	Social Sciences	5,000
3.	Education & General Reference	5,000
4.	Business	4,000
5.	Humanities	4,000

6. Fine Arts	1,000
7. Middle East	1,000
TOTAL	$39,000

This information was made available to everyone involved so questions could be answered or concerns addressed.

Although faculty review was built into the time table and process of making serial cuts, the subject area librarians working with the leader for each group were assigned the responsibility of preparing preliminary lists of titles to be cut. The working file of titles suggested for cancellation was maintained in a card file. Each card included the title of the serial, the subject coverage of the title, the reason for deselection and the subscription price. A deadline date was set for completing this step in the process. After that date an internal review of the suggested cancellations could be made available to all faculty with ample time to respond before the cancellation was ordered. It would not be possible to document all of the changed decisions made throughout the process, but based on how efficiently and effectively the process worked, it should be recommended for other institutions to use if they are faced with the dilemma of serials cancellations.

One of the major factors considered in the deselection process was availability at another library. The importance of cooperative agreements/services throughout the nation becomes much more evident when considering this factor. The need for a national periodicals center (or national periodical system, if that is your preference) becomes much clearer as a library goes through this exercise. The information explosion coupled with declining budgets in inflated dollars is forcing all libraries to rely on the concept of access rather than ownership.

The Library's first level of cooperation is within the University itself. Rather than cancel unique subscriptions, attempts were made to eliminate all duplicate subscriptions on campus, except where high usage made this decision impossible. Since the Marriott Library and the Eccles Health Sciences Library were working on cancellations simultaneously, close coordination permitted cancellation of a significant dollar amount of higher priced serials while still retaining one copy on campus. Holdings at the Law Library also influenced deselection decisions.

The second level of cooperation is at the state level. Special interbrary loan procedures and direct borrowing privileges for students and faculty at all institutions of higher eduction already exist. A shuttle service delivers library materials on a regular basis between Brigham Young University, Utah State University, Universiy of Utah and Weber State College. A serial subscription become a more likely candidate for deselection if the title was held by another institution and especially if their holdings were greater than the University of Utah's.

The University of Utah also draws upon national resources such as the Center for Research Libraries. The unit costs for such services may seem high, but they allow the Marriott Library to avoid purchasing many expensive items while still promising support for the research needs of faculty and students. As stated earlier, it is becoming more apparent that national centers or services must develop if the research needs of each institution are to be satisfied.

In addition to availability of the title, other factors considered were: price, use, curriculum relatedness, interdisciplinary coverage, coverage by indexing services and language of publication. Price was considered in the initial screening process but became a more important factor in the final deselection process and in discussions with faculty. Quite often the decision was made to cancel one costly subscription which would allow retaining two or three other titles. Use of a journal is difficult to determine. The number of times a bound volume has circulated outside the library can be determined by the checkout card, but this does not indicate use within the building. Coverage by indexing services certainly must be (and was) considered since use of the material is greatly determined by access to the contents of journals. Curriculum relatedness is important to consider in the cancellation process; however, in the case of the Marriott Library it was fairly safe to assume that all titles were curriculum-related since we had made cutbacks in subscriptions in 1970--71 and 1973--74. The process of serials cancellations has made the library staff more aware of changes within the University and as a result has learned of new needs and interests that should be supported.

After the final list for cancellation was agreed upon, then orders were issued for cancellation. Many problems arise in making the cancellations since serials have varying expiration dates. You will likely discover that some of the titles you wish to cancel may have just been renewed and paid — especially if you use subscription agents operating under orders to continue subscriptions "until forbidden." Even after final arrangements for cancellations have been made, the task should not be considered as having been completed. Practically every library in the country is housing incomplete runs of serial titles without determining the value of retaining them. For example, what are volumes 3–10 of a title really worth to your library if you are missing the first two volumes and every volume published after volume 10. To solve this problem it is vitally important that libraries, working together through coordinated collections development and resource sharing, try to assure that at least one library is maintaining as complete a backrun as possible. This situation again emphasizes the value of a national periodicals center. A great deal of staff time can be committed to evaluating serials holdings and making decisions on disposal or retention of serial backruns but it is an important responsibility of any library. In the case of the recent cancellations of serials in the Marriott Library the decision has been made to retain the backruns for a period of time in case the decision to cancel was ill-considered. In many of these cases, however, there still may be a gap created between the cancellation date and the reinstatement date.

As a last step in the process, I suggested planning for the future. This planning is not done separately from many decisions already made or planned for with the decision to cancel subscriptions and possibly dispose of backruns of some titles, but should probably be much more comprehensive. If data gathered when preparing a financial or historical analysis supports the need for a larger acquisitions budget, plan your strategy for seeking an increased level of funding. If faculty and researchers have been involved in the serials deselection process, they know why you have had to cancel subscriptions and can be very helpful in supporting budget requests. They are an enlightened silent majority.

The Marriott Library has often used comparative statistical data to support budget requests. Statistical reports provided by the Association of Research Libraries are used not only to show the Library's ranking among all libraries that are members of the Association of Research Libraries, but for comparison purposes with peer institutions selected by the University and accepted by the State Board of Regents. Analysis of this data showed the University of Utah to be near the bottom among peer institutions in expenditures for library materials. Since the State Board of Regents had already accepted the University of Utah's initial goal of being at the 60th percentile among comparable institutions, the Marriott Library prepared a budget request for an increased level of funding. Although this request was not funded by the 1981 Legislature, there is reason for optimism that it will be before long. The graphs in the following tables chart the Marriott Library's change in ranking for several statistical categories during the past ten years. The declining slope of the graphs clearly indicate that the Marriott Library has not maintained an adequate level of support either because the percentage of the institution's budget spent on libraries has decreased or the institution itself has not received as great a level of funding as other institutions, assuming that they have not changed their percentage of support for libraries. Another statistical analysis should be completed to determine this.

In summary, the need to cancel serial subscriptions is not an exercise to look forward to, but faced with the need to do so, plan

UNIVERSITY OF UTAH LIBRARIES
IN RANK ORDER AS COMPARED
WITH ARL LIBRARIES

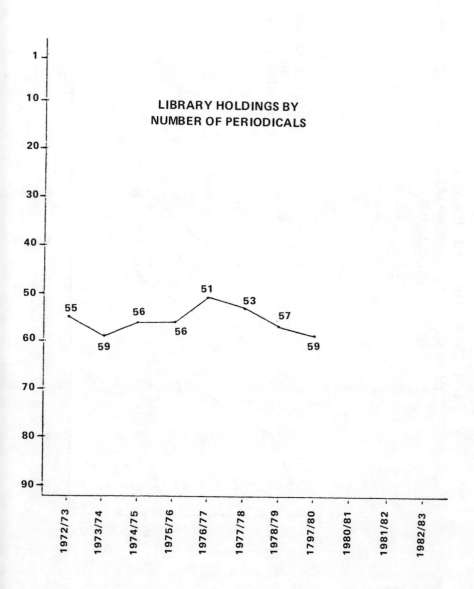

LIBRARY HOLDINGS BY
NUMBER OF PERIODICALS

55

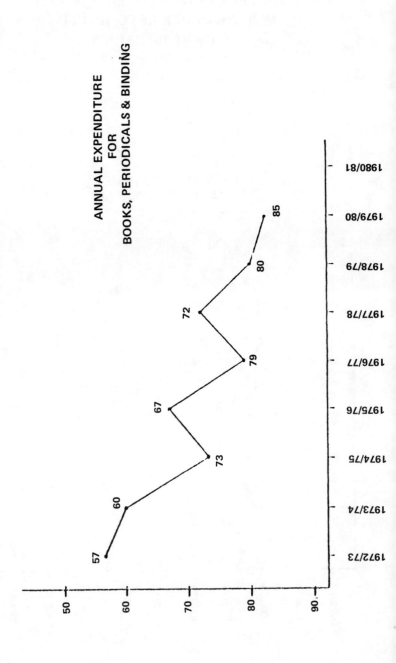

UNIVERSITY OF UTAH LIBRARIES
IN RANK ORDER AS COMPARED
WITH ARL LIBRARIES

ANNUAL EXPENDITURE
FOR
BOOKS, PERIODICALS & BINDING

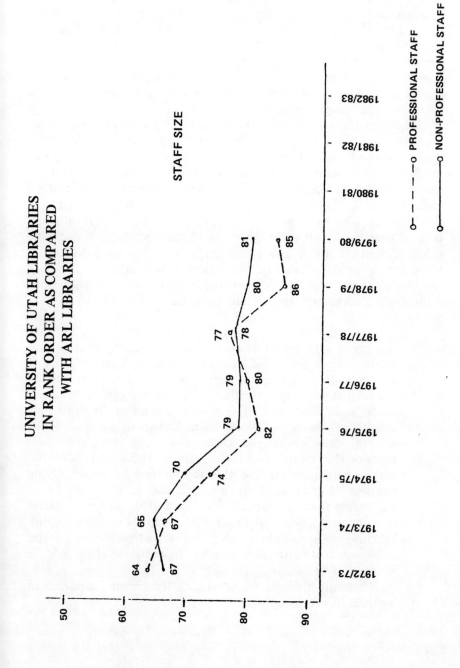

UNIVERSITY OF UTAH LIBRARIES
IN RANK ORDER AS COMPARED
WITH ARL LIBRARIES

STAFF SIZE

o - - - o PROFESSIONAL STAFF

o——o NON-PROFESSIONAL STAFF

57

your procedure and process to gain the greatest input from users to minimize the detrimental effects. Doing this also provides opportunities to change patron's attitudes and understandings. Many librarians understand and accept the principle of access instead of ownership. Most patrons do not. Their attitude, as well as those of some librarians, must change. Having to cancel serial subscriptions can provide convincing evidence of the need for change. Bibliographic access is improving, although more improvement is needed, but improvements in document delivery are not keeping pace with improved bibliographic access.

What are the alternatives to having the material inhouse? Keep yourself (and your users) informed of trends, such as electronic mail. Improved technology provides opportunities but it also poses problems. Who should pay for such services? How do we budget for these services? Is access instead of ownership more applicable to some subject fields than others? It is difficult to imagine anyone in the humanities being satisfied with "a fact" or one "bit" of information. It is also difficult to imagine a university, whose purpose is to teach students to think and to reason, not feeling the need to develop strong local collections. The following quotation from Henry Steele Commager[8] regarding information gathering and scholarship should be a guiding principle to our future decisions.

" . . . until you have read widely and deeply you simply do not know what information you want. Reading in the realm of the humanities — and I suspect, the social sciences — is not a matter of gathering data that you have already decided is essential to your investigation; it is rather a matter of developing ideas, and then of searching around in the most miscellaneous places — few of them known in advance — for relevant data — what the scholar does is to haunt those sections of the library stacks which appear to have the books he wants, pulling down first this volume and then that, trying out one after another, hitting on books he has never heard of, leafing through journals for the most unexpected articles or documents, while ideas ferment. I cannot imagine a scholar going to some library shelf for a particular volume and being content with that volume. Information, like gold, is where you find it.

Certainly there is no substitute for training students to work in this fashion."

References

1. Broude, Jeffrey, "Journal Deselection in an Academic Environment: A Comparison of Faculty and Librarian Choices," *The Serials Librarian*, Vol. 3 (2), Winter 1978.

2. Archer, Stephen H., "The Structure of Management Decision Theory," *Academy of Management Journal*, December 1964.

3. Holley, Robert P., "Serials Cancellations in the Marriott Library," unpublished report prepared for the University of Utah Libraries, Fall 1980.

4. Kuhn, Warren, "Iowa State University Library, Twelfth Annual Report," 1978–79.

5. Toombs, Kenneth, "Report of the Director, University Libraries, University of South Carolina," July 1979 to July 1980.

6. Stuart-Stubbs, Basil, "Report of the University Librarian to the Senate of the University of British Columbia," 1979–80.

7. Brown, Norman and Jane Phillips, "Price Indexes for 1980, *Library Journal*, July 1980.

8. Commager, Henry Steele, "Problems of the University Library," *The Library-College Journal*, Fall 1970.

THE EXPANDED JOURNALS ACCESS SERVICE AT THE CENTER FOR RESEARCH LIBRARIES: ITS IMPACT ON NORTH AMERICAN LIBRARIES

Donald B. Simpson

The Center for Research Libraries is most simply described as a cooperative library for libraries whose basic purpose is to make accessible to its members more library materials for research than they can possibly provide from their own individual collections.

The Center was founded in 1949 by ten major midwestern universities as a means of fostering library cooperation in making infrequently used research materials readily accessible. Because of the inadequacy of their own collections libraries had begun to cooperate by interlibrary loan, but useful as this practice was it was too restrictive and too passive to assure access to any title a library might need that it had been unable to acquire for its own collection. Neither did it do anything to help solve the problem of the continuing growth in the size of each individual collection. What was required was a means by which libraries could effectively coordinate their acquisition programs so that the money they were spending in duplicating the acquisition and housing of infrequently used titles in each of several libraries could instead be spent on acquiring different titles and thus increasing the resources available. Also needed was a means for inexpensive centralized housing of a single copy of the infrequently used titles already in libraries, instead of many libraries each having to continue to house its own copy forever. The most practical and effective solution was recognized to be a cooperatively supported separate institution whose facilities could be built to provide economical housing for large quantities of infrequently used materials. Such a separate institution, with no local readers whom it has a responsibility to serve first, could also arrange its collections and organize its operations so that it could lend everything in its collections quickly and efficiently to other libraries.

For these reasons the founding universities incorporated the Center as a free-standing, non-profit, educational institution whose primary purpose is to help libraries improve and increase the access' they can provide to the books, journals, documents, manuscripts, and all other library materials needed to support research. The logic of this solution, coupled with the commitment to its continuing support by a large group of major universities, encouraged the additional support of the Carnegie and Rockefeller foundations, who together gave $1,000,000 to construct a building designed to serve most efficiently its functions of providing economic housing and fast interlibrary loan. Aside from this initial founding grant and several subsequent grants for special projects from both private foundations and government agencies, the Center has been supported entirely by its member institutions.

Only two significant changes have been made in the Center's organization and policies since its founding. Established as the Midwest Inter-Library Center, it was originally intended to serve only the midwest region. It was assumed one such Center could serve only a limited number of institutions which were in close geographical proximity. This assumption was based on the belief that if too large a number of institutions had access to the materials there would be conflicts between requests. It was further believed that distance would be a significant factor in the service the Center would be able to render. Both of these beliefs proved false. Due to the nature of the material collected conflicts in use occur extremely infrequently. Since the Center is devoted solely to interlibrary lending, it is normally able to get material to requesting libraries within a reasonable time, faster often than they can receive materials from institutions which may be only a few miles from them. Accordingly, in 1961 all geographic restrictions on membership were removed, and in 1965 the name was changed to The Center for Research Libraries to remove any connotation of regionalism.

At about the same time another significant change was effected in the Center's membership policies. Membership had been limited to institutions committed to the support of research on a broad scale, that maintained large libraries of their own, and were interested in buliding a collection of materials beyond that accessible in their own libraries. It was eventually recognized that many institutions which did not meet these criteria still had need for continuing access to the types of material the Center was collecting, though usually on a less frequent basis. Accordingly, in 1968 provision was made for associate membership for institutions whose libraries contained less than 500,000 volumes and that spent an average of less than $200,000 per year for acquisitions.

The Center for Research Libraries now has 118 full members and 66 associate members. In location these span the continent, and beyond, from Harvard University to the University of Hawaii, and from the University of Florida to the University of British Columbia, making the Center not merely a national but an international organization. Most of the full members are universities, but large public libraries and state libraries also belong. The associate members are equally widely distributed through both the United States and Canada and include colleges, public libraries, governmental research institutes, and industrial corporations. Though not in the category of either full or associate members, supporting participants in some of the Center's cooperative microform projects are found literally around the world, in North America, Europe, Asia, Africa, Southeast Asia, and Australia.

The Center's Collections

The Center's collections already include more than three million volumes, and they are constantly being increased. They cover a wide spectrum of subject fields, all forms of publication, and numerous languages, and are formed in two ways: by direct acquisition by the Center through purchase, exchange, and gift; and by deposit by the member libraries. "Deposit" may be a somewhat misleading term, for most member deposits are in fact made with transfer of title to the Center. A smaller number are made as permanent loans; that is, the member retains legal title to the material but it may not withdraw it. In either case the Center undertakes to retain the material in perpetuity. Both the "deposits" and the direct acquisitions thus form a jointly supported central collection, readily accessible to every member by right, and permanently augmenting and extending its own local collection.

The materials in the Center's collections are too diverse and too extensive to be accurately described in a brief statement. An inventory and description of the major categories and classes can be found in the Center's *Handbook*, currently under revision. Of particular importance to most libraries is the Center's program for providing access to currently published journals, with about 14,000 titles now being received. The CRL serials program will be described more fully below.

Special mention should also be made of the very large and rapidly expanding collection of microform copies of records from both public and private archives, particularly from the Public Record Office, in Great Britain, and from the U.S. National Archives; of the large collections, and comprehensive access provided to foreign doctoral dissertations, newspapers, and documents of the U.S. States; and of the many and diversified collections in microform of early and scarce books and journals printed in the U.S., Great Britain, and Europe.

Membership

The Center has two classes of members called, respectively, "Members" and "Associate Members." The class of membership is determined by the characteristics of the library maintained by the institution. Member institutions must maintain a library of more than 500,000 volumes, and spend an average of more than $200,000 per year on acquisitions and binding. Institutions whose libraries do not meet these qualifications are eligible only for Associate Membership. Any university, college, governmental institution, public library, privately endowed library, corporation, or other institution may be considered for full or associate membership, as appropriate, but actual membership can be granted only by vote of the Center's Board of Directors after receipt of a letter of application from the prospective member or associate member.

Since it is the parent institution, and not its library, that is the member or associate member, letters of application must be signed by the chief executive officer of the institution. In universities and colleges this is the president. In industrial or governmental institutions, the letter of application is normally signed by the Director of the laboratory or research establishment served by the library. Only in state libraries, public libraries, or privately endowed libraries is the Director or chief librarian normally regarded as the chief executive officer of the institution.

Both members and associate members have the same rights of access to the Center's collections except that in case of simultaneous requests for the same item the full member's request is given priority.

Members are entitled to two representatives on the Council of the Center. One of these is the head librarian at the institution, the other is any non-librarian appointed by the president. In the case of universities the Center recommends that this non-librarian representative be a senior administrative officer such as the Academic Vice-President, Provost, Dean of the Graduate School, or the Dean of the College of Arts and Sciences. This recommendation is usually followed, but the president may appoint any non-librarian he chooses. Associate members have no representation or vote on the Council.

Membership fees are determined annually by Council of the Center in conjunction with the Center's budget. The present formula for full members provides that 20% of the total to be paid by all full members shall be divided equally among them, and that the remaining 80% shall be divided among them in proportion to each member institution's own average annual expenditures for acquisitions and binding for the last five years. Associate member universities offering the doctorate degree in two or more fields pay on the same formula base as full members, but pay only half the amount they would pay if they were full members.

Member Services

Members and associate members of the Center are entitled to borrow for the use of their readers any material in the Center's collections, regardless of form. Requests to borrow material may be sent on standard ALA interlibrary loan forms, or via collect teletype, telephone and value-added telecommunications networks. When requested via the latter, materials are sent from the Center by United Parcel Service or air parcel post. When requested by mail, the materials are sent by library rate parcel post. Regardless of how shipped by the Center, the borrowing library may return the material by library rate parcel post. The Center bears the cost of shipments from the Center but the borrowing library is expected to prepay the cost of return. Aside from the cost of the return shipment there is no charge to the borrowing member or associate member for any loan.

There is no time limit on loans to members, except that the material is subject to recall after two weeks if needed by another member. Although there is no time limit, members are expected to return the material as soon as the user has finished with it.

There is no limit on the amount of material a member or associate member may borrow at one time, or have on loan at one time. However, since microfilm copies of newspapers are frequently used, loans of these are usually limited to a maximum of twelve reels for any one reader at one time. This means that a library may have many dozens of reels on loan at one time, but each group is for a different reader. If an individual needs to examine a larger number of reels, and the nature of his use is such that he can examine more than twelve reels within a two-week period, upon request the Center will make suitable exceptions to this policy.

Members and associate members may borrow Center materials for any patron they elect to serve. They are not restricted to borrowing only for faculty members and doctoral candidates unless they impose this restriction on themselves. But while materials may be borrowed for the use of an undergraduate student, they are intended for research use and may not be borrowed for either reserve book room use, or use for assigned reading by a class. Libraries are normally expected to buy their own copies for such use.

The Center does not require that materials borrowed from it be used only within the borrowing library. The borrowing library may, at its discretion, lend the materials to its readers for use outside the library.

Since the mid-1950s the members of the Center for Research Libraries (CRL) have been seeking means of utilizing CRL to meet the problem of providing access to periodical literature.

So much has been written about this problem that it need not be detailed here. It may be summarized briefly as resulting from two trends, the proliferation of the number of periodicals published in the world and the increasingly limited financial resources available to libraries in relation to the inflating cost of library materials. The result is that libraries find themselves able to provide rapid and assured access to a steadily decreasing percentage of the world's periodicals.

Recognizing the problem, several programs have been undertaken at the CRL to increase access to periodical literature. From 1956 to 1968 CRL maintained a program, supported in part by the National Science Foundation, to subscribe to journals abstracted in *Chemical Abstracts* and in *Biological Abstracts* that were not commonly held by the members of CRL. Under this program CRL entered subscriptions to about 4,000 titles in the fields of science and technology. Most of these were of foreign origin, with Japanese and Russian journals in particular being present in large numbers. While this program ended in 1968, subscriptions entered under the program have been maintained. In 1959 the Center entered into an exchange program with the Academy of Sciences of the USSR that has led to its receiving all of that institution's serial publications from 1957 to date. It is worth noting that primarily as a result of these two programs, CRL currently receives over 1,140 periodicals from the Soviet Union.

In 1969 the Center for Research Libraries began receiving almost comprehensive coverage of periodicals from South and Southeast Asia through its participation in the Library of Congress cooperative acquisitions programs for those regions. As the cost of maintaining these programs has increased, many members of CRL have been able to cut back on their own participation with the assurance that they would continue to have access to these materials through their membership in CRL.

From 1973 to 1978, CRL was able to expand its periodical holdings with the aid of a grant from the Carnegie Corporation of New York. Subscriptions were entered to periodicals that members cancelled and to newly begun titles recommended by a CRL member. All subscriptions begun under the Carnegie grant were continued after the grant terminated.

Since CRL was unable to subscribe to all titles recommended by members during the period of the Carnegie-supported program, it began a policy of providing members with photocopies obtained from the British Library Lending Division (BLLD) of articles from journals that were recommended for the CRL collection, but to which subscriptions had not been entered. This policy worked out well and in 1975 the CRL's Council approved a program called the Journal Access Service (JAS) under which CRL would provide members with photocopies of journal articles published from 1970 forward in journals devoted to the fields of science, technology, and the social sciences with the exclusion of clinical medicine. JAS forwards any request in scope for a journal article that cannot be filled from CRL's own collection to the BLLD via a computerized telecommunications network. The BLLD sends the requested photocopy by means of airmail directly to the CRL member institution from which the request originated. All expenses are paid for out of the CRL's budget.

As a result of the acquisitions programs described above, CRL currently provides its members and associate members with access to a collection of nearly 14,000 infrequently used and little held journals that it maintains. Through JAS CRL offers a means for providing photocopies to its members, and those associate members offering doctoral degrees in two or more fields, to the vast majority of journals they may need in the fields of science, technology and the social sciences. In fiscal 1979/80 CRL filled approximately 7,000 requests for articles from current journals from its own collection and acquired for its members 43,359 photocopies of articles from BLLD.

CRL Serials Collection

Serial publications form a significant portion of the Center's collection. As of 1980 the Center held approximately 42,000 serial titles excluding government documents.

Of the total number of serial titles held, approximately 14,000 are journal titles received in original format and 470 are newspapers received currently on microfilm or in original format. In the case of both journals and newspapers, the Center's emphasis is on titles that are important for research but apt to be infrequently used in any one library. While member institutions need assured access to these titles, they cannot afford to buy everything for their own collection and normally would have to forego these in order to acquire other titles they need more frequently.

A library with frequent need for a title will of course buy it even if it is in the Center, but most of the titles subscribed to by the Center would simply not otherwise be readily available to North American researchers. As library budgets become tighter and the costs of subscriptions increase, the importance of the Center acquiring infrequently used titles increases.

As would be expected, a high percentage of the journal titles to which the Center subscribes are in foreign languages. In fact, most of the journal titles in English are published in South Asia and acquired through the Center's participation in the Library of Congress' Special Foreign Currency Program. Though the individual journals subscribed to by the Center were selected because they are apt to be infrequently used in any one of the member libraries, these titles as a whole form the most frequently used portion of the Center's collection. A recent use study revealed that journals currently on subscription account for 30% of the total use of the Center's materials. The use by language is interesting. This same study showed that 30% of the current journals borrowed were in Russian, 18% were in English, 16% were in Japanese and 36% were in other languages.

In addition to the journals subscribed to on a regular basis, a sample collection of popular magazines and comic books is maintained. This collection is kept up to date by purchasing a selection of current issues at twice yearly intervals from the stock of the Chicago wholesale distributor. Samples of the most popular titles in a variety of classes are selected. Included in this collection are such titles as *True Police Cases, Secret Romances, Penthouse, Action Comics* and *Batman*. For obvious reasons this collection is stored under lock and key.

Through the deposits of its members, the Center has acquired backfiles in original format of approximately 18,800 journal titles. These are primarily from the 19th and 20th centuries, though many still older files are also included. All subject areas are covered, but the collection is especially strong in the fields of medicine, technology, and religion. In the latter subject a number of long runs of missionary journals are of particular interest for their accounts of the cultures of Africa and Asia at the time of the first extensive European and American penetration of these continents. Examples of such titles included in the collection would be *Mission Field* (London) 1857–1941, which was published by the Society for the Propagation of the Gospel in Foreign Parts, and *Missions Catholiques* (Lyons) 1877–78, 1881–1896, published by the Bureaux de Missions Catholiques. The older medical and technical journals also are of significant historical value. In recent years for example the Center has received a large number of requests for its 19th century photography journals. In fact, the demand for these journals has been such that it has been necessary to microfilm a number of them for which the files were in too poor condition to withstand the heavy interlibrary loan traffic.

A unique advantage of a facility such as the Center is that it makes it possible to bring together in one place incomplete files from several institutions to form a complete or nearly complete file. A program to do this systematically was begun in the early years of the Center, but due to a number of difficulties was not pursued. However, the fact that over a period of time members have deposited their individually incomplete files has led to this happening without any systematic effort. Whenver it is necessary to microfilm a file due to its condition, an effort is always made by the Center to locate and borrow missing portions of the file from other libraries so that whenever possible a complete run of the title can be filmed.

While the Center has been forced in recent years to limit the number of deposits of serial titles due to space problems, it continues to add to the serial backfiles it holds through the direct acquisition of serials in microform. In the case of journals this is usually done through purchase recommendations which are made by one of the member libraries. The acquisitions librarian, collection development officer or other responsible officer at a member institution will re-commend that the Center acquire a title or a collection. A ballot will then be prepared and circulated to the appropriate persons at all full member institutions who then will vote on whether they wish the Center to purchase the title or collection.

As a result of such purchase proposals the Center has acquired a number of microform collections that consists of or include journal runs. These include such microform collections as American Periodi-cals, Series I:1741--1800, Series II:1801--1850, and Series III: Civil War and Reconstruction (University Microforms); English Literary Periodicals of the 17th to 19th Centuries (University Microforms); French Literary Journals (ACRPP); and Britain and Europe since 1945 (Harvester Press) among others. All such collections which the Center has purchased or is purchasing are described in the Center's *Handbook*, and individual serial titles are cataloged and entered in the Center's printed book *Catalogue*. Among the various microform collections acquired as a result of purchase proposals approximately 1,700 journal titles have been added to the collection. Additional titles are added annually. As would be expected these consist for the most part of pre-20th century journals.

Foreign newspapers being received on microfilm from the Li-brary of Congress account for 150 of the 470 newspaper titles cur-rently received at the Center. The countries represented by these 150 titles are Bangladesh, Egypt, India, Indonesia, Israel, Nepal, Pakistan, Poland, Sri Lanka and Yugoslavia. Through the Association for Re-search Libraries' Foreign Newspaper Microfilm Project, which the Center operates for ARL, another 180 foreign newspaper titles from around the world are made available to researchers at institutions which subscribe to the project. The Center also acquires on microfilm on a current basis 67 U.S. general circulation newspapers from major cities. For about half of these titles complete or very substantial backfiles are also held on microfilm. In addition to the general circulation titles, 19 U.S. newspapers intended for black readers and 12 U.S. foreign language newspapers are received currently on microfilm, while another 42 U.S. foreign language newspapers are currently received in original format. In many instances members subscribe to some of the newspaper titles that the Center receives on microfilm, but then discards their hardcopy files after a period of time and depend upon the Center for retrospective access. In this way they provide their patrons with current news items but save the space and expense of retaining bulky newspaper backfiles which are apt to be infrequently needed.

In addition to the current newspaper subscriptions, the Center holds over 3,600 backfiles of newspaper titles either in microform or original format. The newspapers in original format have been acquired through the deposits of members and cover a wide range of countries, languages and periods. Especially noteworthy is the large number of foreign language newspapers published in the United States in the latter years of the 19th century and the first half of the 20th century. Since the files of many of these ethnic newspapers are unique, special efforts have been made to convert deteriorating files to microfilm so that they might be available to future generations of researchers.

The Immigration History Research Center of the University of Minnesota has worked closely with the Center for Research Libraries in this endeavor. For newspapers of all types an effort is made within the limits of budget to replace deteriorating files with microfilm However, as is the case in many libraries, deterioration tends to outstrip available funds.

In order to provide access beyond the present collection, the Center has a policy of trying to provide on microfilm the run of any newspaper, U.S. or foreign, requested by a member institution to satisfy a patron's current research need. This policy is, of course, subject to the limits imposed by the budget and the existence of suitable files which are either on film or available for filming. This policy has the advantage of allowing members to provide their faculty and students access to titles that are essential to the particular research being carried on, but which fall outside their library's particular collection interests.

In order to increase the resources available for the study of particular areas of the world, the Center has established four area study microform projects that are supported by subscribing institutions with a special interest in these areas. These projects are the Cooperative Africana Microform Project (CAMP), the Latin American

70

Microform Project (LAMP), the Southeast Asia Microform Project (SEAM) and the South Asia Microform Project (SAMP). The subscribers to each project elect a committee which determines what the project will acquire. The purpose of the projects is to bring together a cooperatively held pool of microforms of materials related to the particular area of interest. The projects acquire both positive copies of materials which have already been filmed by some other organization as well as film materials which are not already available in microform. In total the four area study microform projects hold over 470 serial titles. This number does not include government publications which are of primary interest to all of the projects or short runs of journals which have been filmed as part of a collection put together by an individual scholar for his or her own research and subsequently made available to the project for filming.

One particularly fruitful endeavor of the projects in regard to serial publications has been their attempt to create a complete file where none was previously known to exist. LAMP, for example, recently completed filming a complete run of the Mexican journal *Siempre!*, 1953–1977, using broken files which exist at the University of California/Los Angeles, the University of Chicago and the University of Wisconsin. To the best of our knowledge LAMP's microfilm copy is the only complete file in North America. Similarly, CAMP has been attempting for several years to locate and film the newsletters and bulletins issued by African liberation groups. This is particularly difficult because the bibliographic record in regard to many of these is virtually nonexistent and publication patterns normally very irregular. Few libraries have anything close to a complete file of any of these titles and for many of them it is impossible even to know what is missing because of the difficulty of knowing what has been published. In order to film what is believed to be a complete file on the Zimbabwe African National Union's *Zimbabwe News* it was necessary to bring together issues from Boston University, Harvard University, the Library of Congress and Northwestern University.[1]

Expanded Journal Access

While The Center for Research Libraries' current journal programs provide access to the vast majority of journal literature being requested, these programs are still inadequate for several reasons:
1. The vast majority of journal articles that The Center for Research Libraries makes available each year are from journals held by the British Library Lending Division. This presents several drawbacks that prevent it from being an ideal arrangement. The BLLD is an agency of the British government and North American institutions

have no input into its future policies or activities. While the BLLD has been highly responsive in the past to North American needs, there is no assurance that it will be able to be as responsive in the future. How secure can North American institutions be in foregoing subscriptions to periodicals that are available only from Great Britain? If all North American libraries turned to it for copies of periodical articles, could the BLLD handle the volume of requests it would than receive? Can the BLLD continue over a period of many decades to provide an international photocopy service at a cost that does not become prohibitive? Added to these uncertainties is the fact that while the turn-around time on requests CRL submits to BLLD is generally good, it would still be faster if the requests could be filled within North America. For these reasons it would seem advantageous for North American institutions to develop a periodical access system that would not depend on an overseas supplier.

2. One of the primary needs of the research libraries that make up the membership of The Center for Research Libraries is that of providing access to those periodicals that though essential when needed, are apt to be infrequently used. It is these journals that research libraries are most likely to be able to forego subscribing to themselves, or cancelling their present subscriptions to, if they can be assured that they are readily available from CRL. These are also the titles that the BLLD might be expected to consider cancelling if financial difficulties arose. Thus, the expansion of CRL's current collection of infrequently held journals is desirable.

The need to increase the CRL collection of infrequently used periodicals seems the most pressing and achievable. Libraries will continue to subscribe to the more frequently used periodicals if at all possible. By CRL expanding its collections of infrequently used titles, its members will receive more immediate relief in regard to their local acquisitions budgets. Many libraries now are cancelling subscriptions to infrequently used periodicals and so the availability of some periodicals is becoming limited. The Center's Journal Access Service and various regional interlibrary loan networks do at the moment provide access to frequently used titles.

The program for expanding the access to journal literature must meet the following criteria:

1. It should be clear as to scope and objectives so that members, associate members and the library community will know exactly what CRL is doing and can easily determine how they will benefit.

2. It should not have an immediate drastic impact on membership assessments. The program should call for expansion based primarily on an increase in memberships and alternative sources of funding.

3. It should be something that CRL can do well without much

72

risk of failure. Adequate staffing should be provided at all phases. The expansion of the program should be closely tied to the availability of building space and development of adequate procedures to handle an increased volume of requests.

4. It should include a method for providing adequate bibliographic access to all journals to which CRL subscribes. All titles should be added to the CONSER data base.

5. As the periodical acquisitions program is gradually expanding, plans should be made for dealing with the concerns of the publishers of periodical literature. An adversary relationship should be avoided.

6. The program should be coordinated with the programs of other organizations providing access to library materials.

Implementation

The scope of the implementation of Expanded Access to Journal Literature is to increase the number of journal subscriptions maintained by The Center for Research Libraries in order to achieve the Program Objectives. Lack of space in the present facility and insufficient financial resources require a systematic implementation of this program in three phases. This approach will allow for the orderly expansion of CRL's journal holdings to the optimal quantity as space and funds become available.

The first phase is restricted by present space limitations that make it impossible to add more than a few hundred titles over the next two or three years required to build a new facility. The number of titles added also will have to depend upon the extent of the potential use of the additional titles. There is currently neither the space nor the available funds for the additional staff that would be necessary to handle a substantially larger volume of requests than at present. If possible, additional titles should be added without additional cost to the membership. This can best be accomplished by shifting funds from payments for photocopies from the British Library Lending Division (BLLD) to maintaining journal subscriptions at CRL.

The second phase is a gradual and continuous addition of journal subscriptions through a carefully planned effort involving space, staff, program (service), and funding requirements. It is important that future developments be carefully planned. This planning should coincide with the continuing expansion of CRL facilities so that once additional space is available, the staff will be able to begin adding new subscriptions in a systematic manner. Consideration should be given to the specific journals which should be added to the CRL collection, the priority order for adding various types of journals, procedures and staff levels for handling the expected volume of requests so as to provide rapid access, and to establishing reliable financial resources.

The third phase, which could occur at any time after phase one, is a contingency plan for the rapid addition of a large number of journal subscriptions and, subsequently, requests as a result of a substantial infusion of external funding or materials support. Again, careful, but nevertheless speculative planning must be done.

The subscriptions to be added over the next two years must lead to no increase in the membership assessments and to the extent possible should lead to a reduction in costs. The titles selected should also add to the special strengths that already exist in the CRL collection so that staff members at member institutions might better understand what to expect to find at CRL and thus have guidance in making local decisions.

Special strength currently exists in the CRL collection of current journals for titles published outside the United States and Canada. With the exception of titles from South Asia and Southeast Asia, these are primarily journals in languages other than English devoted to the fields of science and technology. The collection is particularly strong in journals from the Soviet Union (1,440 titles) and Japan (473 titles). It is logical for CRL to begin to add to its collection by entering subscriptions to foreign language journals. In addition, journals in foreign languages tend to be less frequently used than titles in English and thus members could more easily cancel their own subscriptions to such titles if they had the assurance that they were available from CRL.

In order not to require additional funds from the membership, subscriptions will first be added to those titles in foreign languages that are so frequently requested through the Journals Access Service (JAS) that the amount spent on photocopies from the British Library Lending Division exceeds the cost of an annual subscription. In order to determine the impact of proceedings in this manner, a study[2] was made of all requests filled through JAS in 1979/80. In most instances the cost of obtaining photocopies from BLLD will exceed the cost of a current subscription in any one year only when their current subscription is supported by a backfile. This would mean that if this program is to stay within presently available financial resources, subscriptions can only be added to titles for which requests for the most recent volumes may be expected to cost more when filled through photocopies supplied by BLLD than it would cost to subscribe. This would add only a very few titles to CRL's journal holdings and over a period of time have an insignificant impact on the cost of obtaining photocopies.

As the extent of the backfile needed for subscription cost to offset BLLD cost increases, so does the average subscription cost. This clearly illustrates the fact that the cost of the annual subscription is as much a factor in this equation as is the number of requests for a journal received annually. It costs $7.25 to obtain a photocopy from BLLD. Thus, the cost of BLLD photocopies will exceed the subscription cost of a journal whose annual subscription cost is $20 if only three requests are received for the current volume, while 18 requests would have to be received for a journal costing $200 for BLLD costs to exceed the subscription cost. This is an important consideration since members will want to cancel some of the more expensive titles in order to have an impact on their own financial problems. It seems clear that CRL should not only subscribe to titles whose subscription cost will immediately offset and reduce BLLD costs, but also begin to develop backfiles of titles with higher subscription costs that will begin to significantly reduce BLLD costs only after backfiles for a number of years have been acquired.

In studying 1979/80 JAS requests, titles from non-English language speaking countries for which there were six or more requests were divided into those which the bibliographic sources indicated are entirely in a foreign language and those that contain some articles in English as well as articles in foreign languages.

One hundred twenty of the requested journals contained English articles and 105 did not. Since restricting initial subscriptions to journals that contain no English articles would have only a minor impact, both types of journals should be considered for acquisition in the initial stages of the program.

The amount of funds devoted to new journal subscriptions will not add to the combined JAS budget and that portion of the Acquisitions budget designated for journal subscriptions. Subscriptions will be entered at first only to titles that may be expected to reduce JAS expenditures.

Subscriptions to titles whose subscription cost may be expected to be offset by a reduction in JAS cost only after a backfile of several years is acquired, will be entered when new members join CRL. In FY 1981, approximately 9% of the membership assessments are allocated to journal subscriptions. In order to hold the portion of the total budget devoted to journal subscriptions at this level, no more than 9% of the fees paid by new members will be spent for entering new subscriptions. Thus, for example, if an institution joins CRL and pays a membership assessment of $7,500, a subscription or subscriptions will be entered totally no more than $675.

Beginning in July 1981 CRL will begin entering subscriptions to journals from non-English speaking countries that are primarily in a foreign language or languages, by selecting those titles whose past use leads to the expectation that their subscription cost will be offset by a reduction in the cost of obtaining photocopies from the BLLD. CRL will stay within its current budget by subscribing only at first to those titles whose cost may be expected to be offset by a reduction in JAS cost during the current year and by entering subscriptions to journals that will require several years backfiles to offset BLLD photocopy costs only as new members join CRL.

Based on the study of JAS usage in 1979/80 a list of titles whose possession by CRL would offset BLLD photocopy charges over a period of time is being created. This list will be used not only as a means of establishing priorities for new subscriptions, but will also be circulated to the membership as a means of eliciting backfiles that might serve to reduce BLLD photocopy charges. If adequate backfiles are thus acquired, subscriptions to the deposited titles should be entered using funds made available through new member fees.

Conclusion

CRL is not merely a symbol of cooperation and resource sharing. It is the focal point for research libraries to reassess their own local collection needs and to adjust their subscriptions and acquisitions assured that CRL will have the titles they need. That is more than mere cooperation, it is *commitment.*

CRL is at a crossroads. If its members, who have supported its concept and purpose through years of financial plenty in higher education, fall away now when hard times require an even stronger focus on commitment through local collection reassessment and through the shared collection at CRL, CRL is lost. Most important is the lost cause of research libraries, which I fear will never again be able to meet the challenges of making available the research materials required by our universities and scholars without institutions such as CRL. Other organizations now exist that provide technology, but none do, or plan to, provide resources either directly or through the shared commitment of major research libraries across the continent.

By creating a capacity for action which is critical to the public interest, but which does not now exist, the Center for Research Libraries represents the fulfillment of a national need.

In his 1979 State of the Union Message, President Jimmy Carter reaffirmed the national commitment to new research and technological development:

> The health of American science and technology and the creation of new knowledge is important to our economic well-being, to our national security, to our ability to help solve pressing national problems in such areas as energy,

environment, health, natural resources. I am recommending a program of real growth of scientific research and other steps that will strengthen the Nation's research centers and encourage a new surge of technological innovation by American industry . . . .

The CRL reaches toward the commitment, first recognized by the Congress of the United States in the Higher Education Act of 1965, to provide an essential national capability whereby every university and college, every federal and industrial research establishment, and every community library, wherever it may be located in the nation, will no longer be restricted in its ability to satisfy the research, educational and information needs of its patrons.

References

1. Boylan, Ray, "Serial Publications in the Center for Research Libraries," *Serials Review*, January/March 1979.

2. Center for Research Libraries, *A Study of Journal Titles Requested by CRL Members Through the Journal Access Service in Fiscal Year 1979/80*. (Unpublished.)

BIBLIOGRAPHY

Rodney M. Hersberger

Collection development in libraries has assumed a new meaning and taken a new focus as librarians have been forced to make critical decisions with their acquisitions budgets. Many librarians are now articulating a collection development policy to support their library's mission. The impact of serials and their costs on collection development and library acquisitions budgets force librarians to give serials a major emphasis in collection development.

The following bibliography was selected to propose further background and study for interested readers. To limit the scope and to remain within present realities, this bibliography covers only material published since 1970. As Dean White suggests in his paper, 1969 was the last really good budget year. The entries suggest further reading for the various topics covered in the Conference and are intended to supplement the papers. This Conference was one of the first of its kind to center on a particular aspect of collection development. Therefore, supplemental reading material is limited.

USE AND USER SURVEYS

Eardley, D. "Surveys of Journal Use in the Library of the University of Surrey, 1972–1975; A Methodology," (In International Association of Technological University Libraries. Conference, Louvain, Belgium, 1977. Developing Library Effectiveness for the Next Decade, 1978, p161–171.)

Ford, G. "Research in User Behaviour in University Libraries." *Journal of Documentation* 29(March 1973):85–106.

Goffman, W. "Bradford's Law Applied to the Maintenance of Library Collections," in *Introduction to Information Science* comp. by T. Saracevic Boaker, 1970, p200–203.

Healey, J.S. "Research and the Readers' Guide: An Investigation into the Research Use of Periodicals Indexed in the Readers' Guide to Periodical Literature," *Serials Librarian*, 3(Winter 1978)179-190.

Hodowanac, G.V. "Analysis of Variables which Help to Predict Book and Periodical Use," *Library Acquistions: Practice and Theory*, 4, no. 1(1980):75–85.

Langlois, D.C. "Journal Usage Survey: Method and Application," *Special Libraries*, 64(May–June 1973):239–244.

Line, M.B. "Practical Interpretation of Citation and Library Use Studies," *College and Research Libraries*, 36(September 1975): 393–396.

Line, M.B. "Rank Lists Based on Citations and Library Uses as Indicators of Journal Usage in Individual Libraries," *Collection Management*, 2(Winter 1978):313–316.

Line, M.B. "Rank Lists of Journals Requested on Inter-Library Loan," *Interlending Review*, 6(October 1978):130.

Maxin, J.A. "Periodical Use and Collection Development," *College & Research Libraries*, 40(May 1979):248–253.

Shaw, W.M. "Practical Journal Usage Technique," *College and Research Libraries*, 39(November 1978):479–484.

Tobias, A.S. "Yulecarve Describing Periodical Citations by Freshmen: Essential Tool or Abstract Frill," *Journal of Academic Librarianship*, 1(March 1975):14–16.

Trueswell, R.W. "Article Use and Its Relationship to Individual User Satisfaction," *College & Research Libraries*, 31(July 1970): 239–245.

MARKETING COLLECTION DEVELOPMENT AND SERIALS

Bess, E.B. "Faculty Participation in an Evaluation Review of Low-Use Journals," *Medical Library Association Bulletin*, 66(October 1978):461–463.

Logsdon, R.H. "Librarian and the Scholar: Eternal Enemies," *Library Journal*, 95(September 15, 1970):2871–2874.

Miller, L.A. "Liason Work in the Academic Library," *RQ*, 16(Spring 1977):213–215.

Nelson, J. "Suavity and Sacrifice: Steps to Improved Communication with the Faculty in the Academic Library," *California Librarian*, 34(April 1973):34–44.

Warner, E.S. "Faculty Perceived Needs for Serial Titles: Measurement for Purposes of Collection Development and Management," *Serials Librarian*, 4(Spring 1980):295–300.

Warner, E.S. "Utilizing Library Constituents' Perceived Needs in Allocating Journal Costs," *American Society for Information Science Journal*, 31(November 1979):325–329.

Asleson, R.F. "Microforms: Where Do They Fit?" *Library Resources and Technical Services*, 15(Winter 1971):57--62.

Block, C.E. "Exposing the Consumer to Micrographics: First Steps," *Journal of Micrographics*, 7(May 1974):211--213.

Boss, R.W. "Putting the Horse before the Cart," *Microform Review*, 7(March 1978):78--90.

Carroll, C.E. "Some Problems of Microform Utilization in Large University Collections," *Microform Review*, 1(January 1972):19--27.

Farber, E.I. "Administration and Use of Microform Serials in College Libraries," *Microform Review*, 7(March 1978):81--84.

Feinman, V.J. "Dilemmas and Consequences of Converting Periodical Holdings to Microformat," *Serials Librarian*, 4(Fall 1979): 77--84.

Gray, E. "Microform Concept, an Innovative Approach," *Microform Review*, 1(July 1972):203--205.

Gray, E. "Subscription on Microfiche: An Irreversible Trend," *Journal of Micrographics*, 8(May 1975):241--244.

Gregory, R.S. "Acquisition of Microforms," *Library Trends*, 18(January 1970):373--384.

Martin, R.G. "Microforms and Periodical Mutilation," *Microform Review*, 2(January 1973):6--10.

Martin, M.S. "Promoting Microforms to Students and Faculty," *Microform Review*, 8(Spring 1979):87--91.

Microform Utilization: The Academic Library Environment. Report of Conference held 7--9 December 1970, Denver, ERIC.

Niles, A. "Conversion of Serials from Paper to Microform," *Microform Review*, 9(Spring 1980):90--95.

Scott, P.R. "Scholars and Researchers and Their Use of Microforms," *National Microfilm Association Journal*, 2(Summmber 1969): 121--126.

Veaner, A.B. "On Demand Hard Copies from Microfiche -- A New Service Poential," *Microform Review*, 4(October 1975):247.

Weyhrouch, E.E. "Microforms and Their Place in Academic Libraries," *Kentucky Library Association Bulletin*, 35(January 1971): 15--26.

SERIALS MANAGEMENT, BUDGETS AND COSTS

Buckeye, N.J.M. "Library Serials Committee: How to Balance Decreasing Budgets with Collection Development Needs," *Serials Review*, 1(July 1975):5--7.

Clasquin, F.F. "Financial Management of Serials and Journals through Subject 'Core' Lists," *Serials Librarian*, 2(Spring 1978):287--97.

DeGennaro, R. "Escalating Journal Prices: Time to Fight Back," *American Libraries*, 8(February 1977):69--74.

Fowler, J.E. "Managing Periodicals by Committee," *Journal of Academic Librarianship*, 2(November 1976):230–234.

Gold, S.D. "Allocating the Book Budget: An Economic Model," *College & Research Libraries*, 36(September 1975):397--402.

Goyal, S.K. "Allocation of Library Funds to Different Departments of a University — An Operational Research Approach," *College & Research Libraries*, 34(May 1973):219--222.

Kohut, J.J. "Allocating the Book Budget: A Model," *College & Research Libraries*, 35(May 1979):192–199.

Reid, M.T. "Coping with Budget Adversity: The Impact of the Financial Squeeze on Acquisitions," *College & Research Libraries*, 37(May 1976):266–272.

Stewart, B. "Costs of Providing Access to Periodical Literature in Academic Libraries," *Catholic Library World*, 49(September 1977):70--75.

Weger, H.H. "Serials Administration," *Serials Librarian*, 4(Winter 1979):143--165.

White, H.S. "The Economic Interaction of Scholarly Journal Publishing and Libraries During the Present Period of Cost Increases and Budget Reductions: Implications for Serials Librarians," *Serials Librarian*, 1(Spring 1977):221--230.

White, H.S. "Library Materials Prices and Academic Library Practices: Between Scylla and Charybdis," *Journal of Academic Librarianship*, 5(March 1979):20–23.

White, H.S. "Publishers, Libraries and Costs of Journal Subscriptions in Times of Funding Retrenchment," *Library Quarterly*, 46(October 1976):359--377.

COOPERATIVE PROGRAMS FOR SERIALS

Brewer, K. "Method for Cooperative Serials Selection and Cancellation through Consortium Activities," *Journal of Academic Librarianship*, 4(September 1978):204--208.

Chang, D.M. "Academic Library Cooperation: A Selective Annotated Bibliography," *Library Resources and Technical Services*, 21 (Summer 1976):270–286.

Conference on Resource Sharing. 1976. University of Pittsburgh, Graduate School of Library and Information Science, Dekker, 1977.

Council on Library Resources, *National Periodicals Center Technical*

Development Plan. The Council, 1978. p255.

Cuadra, G.A. "Survey of Academic Library Consortia in the U.S.," *College & Research Libraries*, 33(July 1972):271--283.

DeGennaro, R. "Austerity, Technology, and Resource Sharing; Research Libraries Face the Future," *Library Journal*, 100(May 15, 1975):917--923.

Harrar, H.J. "Cooperative Storage," *Library Trends*, 19(January 1971):318--328.

Hendricks, D.D. "Interuniversity Council Cooperative Acquisitions of Journals," *Texas Library Journal*, 47(November 1971):269--270.

Kaplan, L. "Midwest Inter-Library Center, 1949--1964," *Journal of Library History*, 10(October 1975):291--310.

"National Journal Lending Library," *American Libraries*, 4(January 1973):9--10.

Resource Sharing in Libraries. Pennsylvania Association of Colleges and Universities (and others) April 11--12, 1973. Pittsburgh, Dekker, 1974. 393p.

United States. National Commission on Libraries and Information Science, *Effective Access to the Periodical Literature: A National Program*, prepared by a Task Force on a National Periodicals System. NCLIS, 1977. 92p.

Weber, D.C. "Century of Cooperative Programs among Academic Libraries," *College & Research Libraries*, 37(May 1976):205--221.

Williams, G.R. "Inter-Library Loans: The Experience of the Center for Research Libraries," *Unesco Bulletin for Libraries*, 28 (March 1974):73--78.

"The Research Libraries Group in Brief," *The Research Libraries Group, Inc.*, February 1981.

COLLECTION DEVELOPMENT AND SELECTION OF SERIALS

Background Readings in Building Library Collections, ed. by P. Van Orden. Metuchen, NJ, Scarecrow, 1979.

Bolgiano, C.E. "Profiling a Periodicals Collection," *College & Research Libraries*, 39(March 1978):99--104.

Broadus, R.N. *Selecting Materials for Libraries*. New York, Wilson, 1973. p101--110.

Brown, C.D. *Serials: Acquisition and Maintenance*. Birmingham: Ebsco, 1972. 201p.

Davinson, D.E. *The Periodicals Collection*. 2d ed. Boulder, Westview, 1978. 243p.

Evans, G.E. *Developing Library Collections*. Littleton, CO, Libraries

Unlimited, 1979.

Gellatly, P. "Serials Perplex: Acquiring Serials in Large Libraries," in *Serial Publications in Large Libraries*. Graduate School of Library Science, University of Illinois, Urbana, 1970. p29--47.

Griffiths, S.N. "Journal Purchase and Cancellation: A Brief Look at the Problem in Five British Academic Libraries," *Serials Librarian*, 3(Winter 1978):167--170.

Huff, W.H. "Acquisition of Serial Publications," *Library Trends*, 18(January 1970):294--317.

Johnson, C.A. "Weighted Criteria Statistic Score: An Approach to Journal Selection," *College & Research Libraries*, 39(July 1978):287--292.

Katz, W.A. *Collection Development*. New York, Holt, Rinehart & Winston, 1980. p178--200. (Periodicals.)

Katz, W.A. "Periodical Proliferation; Rejection and Selection," *Catholic Library World*, 37(April 1976):376--379.

Katz, W.A. "Serials Selection," in *Serial Publications in Large Libraries*. Graduate School of Library Science, University of Illinois, Urbana, 1970. p11--28.

Kochtanke, T.R. "Model for Serials Acquisition," *Library Acquisitions: Practice and Theory*, 4, no. 2(1980):141--144.

Koenig, M.E.D. "On-Line Serials Collection Analysis," *American Society for Information Science Journal*, 31(May 1979):148--153.

Kraft, D.H. "Journal Selection Model and Its Implications for a Library System," *Information Storage and Retrieval*, 9(January 1978):1--11.

Kraft, D.H. "Journal-Worth Measure for a Journal-Selection Decision Model," *Collection Management*, 2(Summer 1978):129--139.

Osborn, A.D. *Serial Publications: Their Place and Treatment in Libraries*. 2d ed. Chicago, ALA, 1973. 434p.

Rush, B. "Journal Disposition Decision Policies," *Journal of the American Society for Information Science*, 25(July 1974):213--217.

Schloman, B.F. "Retention Periods for Journals in a Small Academic Library," *Special Libraries*, 70(September 1979):377--383.

Seymour, C.A. "Weeding the Collection: A Review of Research on Identifying Obsolete Stock: Serials," *Libri* 22, no. 3(1972):183--189.

Stewart, B. "Periodicals and the Liberal Arts College Library," *College & Research Libraries*, 36(September 1975):371--378.

Use of Library Materials: The University of Pittsburgh Study, by A. Kent and others. Dekker, M., 1979. 272p.

Wenger, C.B. "Journal Evaluation in a Large Research Library," *American Society for Information Science Journal*, 28(September

1977):293–299.

White, H.S. "Factors in the Decision by Individuals and Libraries to Place or Cancel Subscriptions to Scholarly Journals," *Library Quarterly*, 50(July 1980): 287–309.

Woodward, A.M. "Factors Affecting the Renewal of Periodical Subscriptions: A Study of Decision Making in Libraries with Special Reference to Economics and Interlibrary Lending," *Aslib*, 1978. 118p.

INDEX